POEMS *for* ARCHITECTS

POEMS *for* ARCHITECTS

an anthology

Jill Stoner

WILLIAM STOUT PUBLISHERS, SAN FRANCISCO

William Stout Publishers
530 Greenwich Street
San Francisco, CA 94133

Distributed in North America by:
RAM Publications and Distribution
2525 Michigan Avenue, A2
Santa Monica, CA 90404
310.453.0043
310.264.4888
rampub@gte.net

This publication was supported in part by a generous grant from The LEF Foundation.

ISBN 0-9709731-0-1

Library of Congress Control Number: 2001132922

Printed in Hong Kong.

PREFACE

BEFORE I STUDIED ARCHITECTURE I studied poetry, which is to say, I read and thought about a lot of poems. I tried to write some too, but failed; perhaps I did not try hard enough. In any case I became an architect, and for the past twenty years I have turned to poetry to help me define what that might mean.

For me, it does not mean making new buildings. Our landscape is full of a half century of mistakes; I believe that our job now is to clean up the mess. This may not be an aesthetic problem so much as a political one—the unfortunate result of arrogance and of wealth misspent. For such strong statements I can certainly be accused of an arrogance of my own; but in this book, I have tried to let the voices of others speak more loudly than mine.

Poems for Architects is partly a dialogue between me and the authors whose thoughts I often turn to: Paul Valéry, Octavio Paz, Adrienne Rich, Mark Strand. But even more, it is a conversation among the poets themselves; it is each poem speaking to the others. In the selection and the order of the poems I have tried to orchestrate my thoughts through the intoxicating voices of twenty-nine poets who wrote during the twentieth century. In the essays, a few poets from the nineteenth century chime in; their hindsight adds value to what these poems have to say to us today.

One rule I set for myself at the beginning of the project: all of the poems had to come from my own bookshelf. Otherwise, the task of their selection would have been too daunting, the range of possibilities too vast. Some readers will no doubt wonder at certain omissions, and will hopefully extend this anthology implicitly through their reading of other poems.

Reading is that act which, to my mind, most eloquently represents our shared humanity. The collected photographs in André Kertész's *On Reading* affirm how spatial, and how ubiquitous, the act of reading is; they exactly suit the spirit in which I want to introduce the five sections of this book. The drawings of the villanelles are my own attempt to hold the inexorable tide of computer drafting at bay—the process of making these drawings greatly extended my pleasure in the content and structure of those poems.

I discovered that the writing of a book has phases not unlike the phases of the architectural design process—the exhilaration of schematic design (over in a flash), and then what seem like endless revisions to red-lined construction documents. Like many naïve designers, I had no idea how much of the task of making a book came after the design, how much was a matter of detailing. In this, as in all other parts of this writing journey, I have had much help, and would like to extend thanks:

To the University of California at Berkeley, for sabbatical time; to the LEF Foundation, for generous financial support; to Robert Gurbo and the Kertész Foundation, for permission to use the photographs; to Robin Stoner, for time and space in the mountains; to Susannah Meek, Kris Liberman, Sarah Stoner-Duncan, and Ben Stoner-Duncan for the kind of support which required generosity and sacrifices; to Susan Ubbelohde, Donlyn Lyndon, Nick Ragouzis and Karen Ostrow, for their valuable criticism; to Sarah Granatir, for her patience and incredibly fine judgment; to Peter Schneeman and David Buege, for intellectual friendship much deeper than intellect, and for their exactitude; to Bill Stout, for the leap of faith.

To Mac Miller, who first got me drunk on poetry, this book is dedicated.

Jill Stoner

San Francisco, August 2001

CONTENTS

WHY POEMS?

The poet can never see too much or feel too much. His metaphors are only ways of getting rid of the dead white plaster of the cupola.

Ernest Fenollosa

WHY SHOULD ARCHITECTS READ POEMS, and how might they be useful? According to Vitruvius, delight itself is useful, but poems do more than delight. They draw us into the tiny spaces within the letters and between the words; they make rooms of stanzas and roofs of rhyme. The forty-eight poems in this collection invite us in, to make use of them in any way we choose.

Some of these poems speak to us directly about the places we inhabit—our rooms and our cities. Others describe more abstract structures, through both their content and their form. The lessons we can learn from them do not come through interpretation. In fact, 'lessons' and 'learn' may be the wrong words —these poems can enter our sensibility directly, without a detour through the mind. Paul Valéry calls poetry "a universe of language that is not the common system of exchanging signs for acts or ideas."[1] Implicitly he suggests that, though structured of words, poetry may share more qualities with music and dance than with the other literary arts.[2]

In his poem "Ars Poetica" Archibald MacLeish gives this enigmatic rule for the verbal art of poetry:

A poem should be palpable and mute
As a globed fruit.

Palpability suggests weight. The Indo-European root of the word *poetry* is *kwei*, meaning *to pile up, to build*, whence the Greek word *poiein, to make* or *create*, whence *poet* and *poem*. One of the first technologies was this 'piling up' of words. To further muddy the etymological waters, the word *technology* shares its Indo-European root *teks*, meaning *to weave* or *to fabricate*, with the word *architecture*. According to these ancient roots, the poet is the builder whose art responds to weight, while the architect is the weaver of the text.[3]

How might a poem have weight? Octavio Paz seems to contradict MacLeish when he says that a poem is "a thing made of words, for the purpose of containing and secreting a substance that is *impalpable,* resistant to definition."[4] Unlike the buildings of architects, which take up physical space, no single poem precludes the existence of any other. If we burn the book, the poem continues to exist. Poems do not occupy space; they create it. Palpable or not, poetry is language squeezed to its essence, it is words made rich through a runic economy of means. As for being mute, both Paz and MacLeish would agree that the poem refuses to give us answers.

'Answers' are what an architect receives at the beginning of each project, in the form of:

a program of spaces
a budget
a site map
a code book.

These elements mask their abstract potential with seemingly useful underpinnings that quantify and schedule our tasks. In fact, our real task is to compose of these disparate perspectives a common root 'poem' consistent with our time. This collection is devoted to the poetry of the twentieth century, a century marked by the acknowledgment of uncertainty, of change, and of the limits of knowledge. Such inconsistencies demand a lighter touch; with their weighty words, poems now challenge architecture to 'lighten up.'

In 1967, the landscape architect Lawrence Halprin sought to provoke the design professions with this thought: "Our utilitarian notions have to give way in the face of the demands of our unconscious psyche."[5] Arranging his words differently, we might today ask: "Faced with the daunting utilitarian demands of our profession, how do we transcend that which we cannot ignore?" My premise is that poems can help. They provide *inspiration*, a word trivialized through overuse but meaning, simply, *to breathe into*. It is easy to think of reading a poem in this way—the lines are designed to coordinate with the breath. When we 'breath in' these magically orchestrated words, the words nourish our thought. Modern poems are food for design.

The resonance between Homeric epics and Greek temples is straightforward —they tell the same story in two different forms. Both modern poetry and modern architecture have professed to relinquish the function of storytelling. According to Valéry, the modern poem "exacts from us a participation that is nearer to complete action."[6] Like an active verb, it places us in the role of the subject. Yet a poem also slows time down. In "Ars Poetica" MacLeish goes so far as to call for a poem to "be motionless in time," perhaps so motionless that it transforms time into space.

The space of poetry reflects the space of life; yet the modern poem is more than reflective; it is instrumental, and exists to be acted upon. Valéry tells us that "A poem is really a kind of machine,"[7] reminding us of Le Corbusier's 1924 redefinition of house as a "machine for living in."[8] The word *machine* can be traced to its root *magh*, meaning *to have power*, a root that also gives us the word *magic*. The magic of the poem *is* its power.

Complementing the poem-as-machine is the experience of the poem; the poem also acts upon us. *Experience* shares its word root with *peril*. In whatever quotidien guise, danger is lurking everywhere, and it is this that gives the spaces of our daily life, the spaces of the house and the city, their charged reality. The poem takes us to the space at the periphery of consciousness, the space we see and almost grasp in a moment like that between sleep and waking. Like dreams, poems allow us to confront these fearsome spaces; yet when we build, it is to shelter ourselves from the dark places of poems and dreams.

Reality is a cliché
From which we escape by metaphor.
Wallace Stevens

THE KINGDOM OF POETRY is landscaped with many species of literary device, but none flourishes so inexorably as metaphor. As defined by Aristotle, metaphor consists in "giving one thing a name that belongs to another." This conferring is a form of transportation (in Athens, the public transit vehicles are called *metaphorai*) in which the reciprocity between things is often symmetrical. Sleep can be a metaphor for death, but so can death be a metaphor for sleep.[9] Metaphor narrows the gap; it spans between two things. It provides conveyance from the space of one thing to the space of another, but unlike the Athens streetcar it does so by *diminishing* distance.

When Robert Lowell writes "You asked for evening, it descends, it's here; Paris is coffined in its atmosphere" we have the metaphor of the city as a body, of the air as an enclosure, of the night as death. These lines are from one of Lowell's sonnets to Charles Baudelaire, and the infinite number of such correspondences and patterns are what Baudelaire meant when he referred to life itself as a "forest of symbols."[10] In poetry as in life, there are many ways to explore this forest; poets and teachers often advocate multiple readings of a poem to reach its various levels. I would say that architects can read a poem in at least four ways: the first two are for sensation and content, the third is for the form within the content, and the fourth is to uncover the formal properties of the poem itself. The sections in this book lend themselves, roughly, to these four ways of reading.

First, we may read a poem intuitively, and in such a reading the images within the poem resonate immediately through connection with our own experience. "Poems at Home" is a narrative of domesticity, in which the personal interior becomes variously an empty container, a container of nostalgic yearning, and a container of memory. Some of the sites are urban, some suburban, and some rural, but all these poems are about *withinness*. Inside their rooms 'time' frequently appears as an active character, conjuring past, present and future in enigmatic patterns of memory and clairvoyance.

The second mode of reading is as a citizen of a collective or cultural experience that we can define as 'urban.' The poet Lawrence Ferlinghetti recently wrote: "A poem is a mirror walking down a street full of visual delight," which is to say that the poem reflects the patterns of our shared urban experience through words. In the "City Poems," reflected patterns proliferate: human patterns of crowded streets, the rhizome-like[11] patterns of scaffolding and towers, the insidious yet hopeful patterns of infiltrating nature.

The third kind of reading goes yet deeper, and provokes us to excavate a more abstract meaning shaped by the poem as a whole. Poems in the section "The Jar & the Field" illustrate the quixotic spatial paradigms of the century during which the concept of relativity was born. This series begins with the single object that can, by its central and static position, organize the landscape around it into a hierarchical order; it ends with a description of a field that is held together not by substance, but by subjective motion. Through these poems, we can begin to imagine new 'radical', or 'root' forms of space.

"What is form for anyone else is content for me,"[12] writes Valéry on the subject of his own poetry. I suggest that for the fourth kind of exploration we read the poems with an architect's eye, and use our tectonic imagination to distill the formal qualities of the poem through scansion[13] and other diagrammatic devices. Because it is for me the most architectural of the 'closed' forms,[14] I have chosen six villanelles through which to illustrate the possibilities for invention that exist within their strict order. For an architect, this graphic reading is like coming back to the familiar surface of form after diving into the murky depths of content.

Before these four sections, I present three poems as an introduction to the complex relationship between poetry and architecture; I hope that these also, without comment, help to answer the question "Why Poems?"

All the world may be a stage
But for me the world became a page.
William Gass

THE MARKS ON THE PAGE are the tectonic shadow of the poem, a shadow cast by the architecture of thought. But Mark Strand's two villanelles are not shadows of Giorgio de Chirico's paintings; rather, each painting is the shadow of a poem not yet written. Architecture's own shadow has grown long with the burden of twentieth century doubts and miscreations, and finally the very definition of our art awaits transformation. A simple critique might go something like this:

Architecture is normally heavy; it can also be light.
Architecture is normally visual; it can also be evanescent.
Architecture is normally spatial; it can also be temporal.

Thus I suggest that we look toward poetry to help us locate and express qualities of lightness, of ephemera, and of change. To my way of thinking, this is the gift that one art can now have the pleasure of bringing to another.

Architecture helps to define our relationships to each other and to the world of nature. Metaphysically, it also defines our relationship to our past. The poems in this book address all three kinds of relationships—the stone fences that "make good neighbors," the clearing in the forest that "can only be found by those that have gotten lost," the places "where generations lie / side by side with each other"—and invite architects to enter into these relationships more directly, more passionately, but also with more humility.

In his introduction to the anthology *The Best American Poetry 1991*, Strand tells us why he gave his poems to his father after his mother had died: "He can read my poems...and be in possession of his loss, instead of being possessed by it."[15] The poem cannot change the condition of loss, but it can transform the object of that loss into its subject.

In recent decades many an architectural excess has been committed in the name of poetry, but not on account of the reading of poems. Now we have become disenfranchised of the spaces that are supposed to belong to us; they possess us with alarming authority, and imprison us in symbolic forms that have lost their meaning. These forms are not mute; instead they speak in tongues that we cannot understand. The strange spaces inside poems can, paradoxically, make more familiar the spaces of the daily life; so architects, by visiting these spaces, can become more tuned to the walls we still build, and within which we pass these present days.

Mark Strand

EATING POETRY

Ink runs from the corners of my mouth.
There is no happiness like mine.
I have been eating poetry.

The librarian does not believe what she sees.
Her eyes are sad
and she walks with her hands in her dress.

The poems are gone.
The light is dim.
The dogs are on the basement stairs and coming up.

Their eyeballs roll,
their blond legs burn like brush.
The poor librarian begins to stamp her feet and weep.

She does not understand.
When I get on my knees and lick her hand,
she screams.

I am a new man.
I snarl at her and bark.
I romp with joy in the bookish dark.

Wallace Stevens

THE HOUSE WAS QUIET AND THE WORLD WAS CALM

The house was quiet and the world was calm.
The reader became the book; and the summer night

Was like the conscious being of the book.
The house was quiet and the world was calm.

The words were spoken as if there was no book,
Except that the reader leaned above the page,

Wanted to lean, wanted much most to be
The scholar to whom his book is true, to whom

The summer night is like a perfection of thought.
The house was quiet because it had to be.

The quiet was part of the meaning, part of the mind:
The access of perfection to the page.

And the world was calm. The truth in a calm world,
In which there is no other meaning, itself

Is calm, itself is summer and night, itself
Is the reader leaning late and reading there.

W. H. Auden

PROLOGUE: THE BIRTH OF ARCHITECTURE

(for John Bayley)

From gallery-grave and the hunt of a wren-king
    to Low Mass and trailer camp
is hardly a tick by the carbon clock, but I
    don't count that way nor do you.
already it is millions of heartbeats ago
    back to the Bicycle Age,
before which is no *After* for me to measure
    just a still prehistoric *Once*
where anything could happen. To you, to me,
    Stonehenge and Chartres Cathedral,
the Acropolis, Blenheim, the Albert Memorial
    are works by the same Old Man
under different names: we know what He did,
    what, even, He thought He thought,
but we don't see why. (To get that, one would have
    to be selfish in His way,
without concrete or grapefruit.) It's our turn now
    to puzzle the unborn. No world
wears as well as it should but, mortal or not,
    a world has still to be built
because of what we can see from our windows,
    that Immortal Commonwealth
which is there regardless: It's in perfect taste
    and it's never boring but
it won't quite do. Among its populations
    are masons and carpenters
who build the most exquisite shelters and safes,
    but no architects, any more
than there are heretics or bounders: to take
    umbrage at death, to construct

a second nature of tomb and temple, lives
    must know the meaning of *If*

Postscript

Some thirty inches from my nose
The frontier of my Person goes,
And all the untilled air between
Is private *pagus* or demesne.
Stranger, unless with bedroom eyes
I beckon you to fraternize,
Beware of rudely crossing it:
I have no gun, but I can spit.

POEMS AT HOME

And as imagination bodies forth
The forms of living things unknown, the poet's pen
Turns them into shapes, and gives to airy nothing
A local habitation and a name.

William Shakespeare

HOME IS NOT A MODERN IDEA—Odysseus's twenty-year journey is the quintessential mythic representation of the longing to be 'at home.' In *The Odyssey*, Ithaca is the object of yearning; it is 'out there' like a pastoral landscape or a lover, a magnetic jewel hanging at the horizon of the hero's imagination and pulling him forward through the extraordinary sequence of perils that seem to be the subject of the story. In fact, the subject of *The Odyssey* is *home*; the ideal of Ithaca validates all the episodes that lead there.

Two American writers of the nineteenth century present to us the opposite condition—the absence of longing through being 'at home.' In 1841, Henry Thoreau went to live at Walden Pond in order to demonstrate that home can be as simple as the manifestation of extreme economy (he built his house for $28) and absolute privacy: "My dwelling was small, and I could hardly entertain an echo in it."[16] His writing may have soon had an influence: a couple of decades later and elsewhere in Massachusetts, a similar spirit of home entered the house of poetry through Emily Dickinson.

Like Thoreau, Dickinson lived hermetically; Adrienne Rich writes of her: "Probably no one ever lived so much and so purposefully in one house; even, in one room."[17] This room was on the corner, with good light and high ceilings, furnished with a bed and a small table with one drawer. At this table Dickinson composed most of her 1,700 poems, and as legend has it she wrote while wearing nightclothes. Her letters reveal her commitment to solitude as a matter of choice: "I'm afraid I'm growing selfish in my dear home, but I do love it so."[18] In fact, her seclusion within that single chamber manifests a desire to live in a house more like Thoreau's cabin, more intimate than grand. Her room, not her father's mansion, was 'home.'

She wrote from home but not about home—her attention was focused outward on that which she could not see—flowers, children, the mountains and the ocean, the metaphysics of life and death. Being at home magnified and clarified the world outside; for her the mind's vision was sharper than the eye:

> I never saw a moor,
> I never saw the sea;
> Yet know I how the heather looks,
> And what a wave must be.

In her letters and poems, the house figures as a metaphor for nature and art:

> Nature is a haunted House, but art is a house that tries to be haunted.[19]

for death:

> Safe in their alabaster chambers,
>   untouched by morning and untouched by noon,
> Sleep the meek members of the resurrection;
>   Rafter of satin and roof of stone.

and for poetry itself:

> I dwell in Possibility
> a fairer House than Prose—
> More numerous of Windows—
> Superior—for Doors—

Dickinson's poems make it possible for *us* to dwell in the house of ordinary images. They elevate the common noun, and bear out the assertion of William Carlos Williams more than a half century later that meaning resides "[not in] ideas but in things."[20] Williams was a physician by profession; perhaps this in some way extended his imagination to the visceral beauty of ordinary objects. His "red wheelbarrow / glazed with rainwater / beside the white chickens" [21] set a didactic example for modern poetry to celebrate the artifact that stands only for itself.

Unfortunately, advertising has proved more powerful than poetry in channeling our national appetite for things, and one of the challenges for architecture during this mediacentric time is to separate the *object* from the *commodity*. The object offers itself for contemplation, the commodity for consumption. The object self-renews, the commodity gets used up. Marketing has extinguished the sparks of subtlety that give an ordinary thing its resonance; it has convinced us that we need to be offered our wheelbarrow in a variety of colors. Common nouns and modifiers in the following poems catalogue the domestic contents of cellars and attics, the colors of facades and furnishings, and the elemental fabric of the house itself—in fact, the ordinary stuff of which architecture is made.

The private individual, who in the office has to deal with realities, needs the domestic interior to sustain him in his illusions...In the interior, he brings together remote locales and memories of the past.

Walter Benjamin, "The Interior, the Trace"

THE DOMESTIC INTERIOR IS BOTH the space of introspection and a metaphor for introspection. Edgar Allen Poe, with the invention of the detective story, transferred the site of fantastic literature from the landscape of the future to the landscape of the mind. His stories develop the interior of the house as a parallel to the subconscious self; many play out the drama wherein dark rooms and darkness of mind intermingle. When the House of Usher crumbles, 'house' holds a double meaning; it is both the family structure and the physical structure that collapse. This resonance between the self and the house is the subject of many of these "Poems at Home."

Langston Hughes brings into focus the semantic distinction between house and home[22]—the one a mere shell awaiting the other. We can compare his poem "Empty House" to these lines by Emily Dickinson:

> I know some lonely houses off the road
> A robber'd like the look of,—
> Wooden barred,
> And windows hanging low.

The house evokes the home only when it is occupied; empty, it may invite the intruder, but to the visitor it contains "more pain than a cutting knife." Home (not house) is an antidote to pain, and many of these poems present the essential comfort of home though memory and through intimacy.

Nowhere has the intimate metaphysics of home been so thoroughly explored as in Gaston Bachelard's *Poetics of Space*. Since its publication in 1958, its philosophical rather than sociological foundation has become a valuable complement to other, more rational theories of domesticity. Drawing extensively from French poetry, Bachelard presents the phenomenology of the house at two scales: first as an *oneiric*[23] or dreamlike space defined primarily by its vertical dimension, and then as a shelter within the larger and more hostile landscape.

The house allows us to be intimate with our own past; it literally shelters time in its numerous small spaces, which are distributed vertically:

> Of course, thanks to the house, a great many of our memories are housed, and if the house is a bit elaborate, if it has a cellar and a garret, nooks and corridors, our memories have refuges that are all the more clearly delineated.[24]

Within the landscape, and as a refuge against hostile weather, the house itself acquires such human qualities that we can become intimate *with* it as well as *within* it:

> Faced with the bestiality of the storm and the hurricane, the house's virtues of protection and resistance are transposed into human virtues. The house acquires the physical and moral energy of a human body.[25]

For Bachelard, the house is anthropomorphic, and its vertical components are unequivocally gendered; he confirms mythic traditions from all over the globe that associate the fecund earth with the feminine spirit and the cerebral atmosphere with the masculine when he says: "It is possible, almost without commentary, to oppose the rationality of the roof to the irrationality of the cellar."[26] Yet W. H. Auden presents an opposite engendering in a pair of poems from the collection *About the House*. "Down There," dedicated to his friend Irving Weiss, suggests that for men, the cellar has a magnetic attraction, where "sometimes to test their male courage, / A father sends the younger boys to fetch something." The poem "Up There" is dedicated to Irving's wife Anne, and begins: "Men would never have come to need an attic," implying that men are entirely rational creatures, and that "only women cling to / Items out of their past they have no use for." Jorge Luis Borges' poem "Inventory" is also about the attic, and though he attaches no gendered reading to the space, he confirms that all these various items amount only to "the accumulation of disorder." In the attic, space and time conjoin; it is impossible to separate these objects from the memories that they invoke.

In the poems that follow, 'time' appears, chameleon-like, in many tenses. James Merrill's "The World and the Child" opens with the image of a father "tiptoeing out backwards" from his son's upstairs room. Time passes in the poem, but the child "does not move," and we are given the impression that two parallel conditions of time exist within the same house. In "House" and "Home" Diana O'Hehir contrasts the present tense mood of Merrill's narrative with a 'tense' of memory. She translates the sheltering plane of a roof into a palimpsest, an abstract "roofline" like a child's drawing on a white page. Her houses are "as transparent as Corinth," where "all that remains is a white space." They are the ghosts of home.

Adrienne Rich writes, by her own account, in response to what she calls a "historical emergency."[27] "In the Wake of Home" begins with ordinary domestic things: "bluegreen curtains / posters and a pile of animals on the bed." As the narrative unfolds, the scope of home gets larger until we finally understand that for her, home is equivalent to the world. She challenges the complacency of the private domestic life by invoking "diasporas unrecorded / undocumented refuges / underground railroads." Before we can fully appreciate what has happened, this long poem has called us to arms.

The poem is the vigil.
Adrienne Rich

BEING VIGILANT IMPLIES BEING SOMETIMES SILENT, giving other voices room. Jacqueline Osherow's villanelle animates the normally inanimate objects that keep us domestic company through the night. Like the lively implements that so astound the sorcerer's apprentice, these things surprise us when they turn the repetitive lines of the villanelle into their own voice: "*Call it,* the refrigerator hums at night / *Call it back, it's drifting,* mourns the streetlight." In an equally charged transformation, John Updike turns his suburban neighbor's house into a source of colorful pleasure through a series of improbable reflections.

Among other things, the American suburb is guilty of propagating sameness; not a sameness of culture, which has always been the glue that holds societies together, but a sameness of commodity, which engenders envy, greed, and even paranoia. In Mark Strand's "The Tunnel" the speaker is psychologically trapped by a man standing outside his house. He "destroys the living room furniture / to show [he] owns nothing of value." We descend again to the basement, this time to "dig a tunnel to a neighbor's yard." In this darkly ominous poem Strand paradoxically reinforces the sense of isolation through the proximity of one house to another. "I feel I'm being watched / and sometimes I hear / a man's voice / but nothing is done / and I have been waiting for days."

The neighbor's yard, flat and ubiquitous, provides no refuge, but the dense wilderness under the freeway makes a haven for O'Hehir's "mad old lady under the ledge." She carves her home deep into the undergrowth, where "the air is as solid as a honeydew melon;" she is an earthy magician who makes domestic space out of nature's leftovers. In "Geometry," Rita Dove invokes a different kind of magic; her windows "hinge into butterflies" and her walls "clear themselves of everything but transparency." Hers is an alternate vision of objects to the one of William Carlos Williams—not to simplify into their most solid form, but to disappear. Contemporary architecture now struggles with just this desire: to make materials lighter than themselves.

Langston Hughes

EMPTY HOUSE

It was in the empty house
That I came to dwell
And in the empty house
I found an empty hell.

Why is it that an empty house,
Untouched by human strife,
Can hold more woe
Than the wide world holds,
More pain than a cutting knife?

W. H. Auden

DOWN THERE

(for Irving Weiss)

A cellar underneath the house, though not lived in,
Reminds our warm and windowed quarters upstairs that
Caves water-scooped from limestone were our first dwellings,
A providential shelter when the Great Cold came,
Which woke our feel for somewhere fixed to come back to,
A hole by occupation made to smell human.

Self-walled, we sleep aloft, but still, at safe anchor,
Ride there on caves; lamplit we dine at street level:
But, deep in Mother Earth, beneath her key-cold cloak,
Where light and heat can never spoil what sun ripened,
In barrels, bottles, jars, we mew her kind commons,
Wine, beer, conserves and pickles, good at all seasons.

Encrust with years of clammy grime, the lair, maybe,
Of creepy-crawlies or a ghost, its flagstoned vault
Is not for girls: sometimes, to test their male courage,
A father sends the younger boys to fetch something
For Mother from down there; ashamed to whimper, hearts
pounding,
They dare the dank steps, re-emerge with proud faces.

The rooms we talk and work in always look injured
When the trunks are being packed, and when, without warning,
We drive up in the dark, unlock and switch lights on,
They seem put out: a cellar never takes umbrage;
It takes us as we are, explorers, homebodies,
Who seldom visit others when we don't need them.

W. H. Auden

UP THERE

(for Anne Weiss)

Men would never have come to need an attic.
Keen collectors of glass or Roman coins build
Special cabinets for them, dote on, index
Each new specimen: only women cling to
Items out of their past they have no use for,
Can't name now what they couldn't bear to part with.

Up there, under the eaves, in bulging boxes,
Hats, veils, ribbons, galoshes, programs, letters
Wait unworshiped (a starving spider spins for
The occasional fly): no clock recalls it
Once an hour to the household it's a part of,
No Saint's Day is devoted to its function.

All it knows of a changing world it has to
Guess from children, who conjure in its plenum,
Now an eyrie for two excited sisters,
Where, when Mother is bad, her rage can't reach them,
Now a schooner on which a lonely only
Boy sails north or approaches coral islands.

Jorge Luis Borges, translated by *Alastair Reid*

INVENTORY

To reach it, a ladder has to be set up. There is no stair.
What can we be looking for in the attic
but the accumulation of disorder?
There is a smell of damp.
The late afternoon enters by way of the laundry.
The ceiling beams loom close, and the floor has rotted.
Nobody dares put a foot on it.
A folding cot, broken.
A few useless tools,
the dead one's wheelchair.
The base for a lamp.
A Paraguayan hammock with tassels, all frayed away.
Equipment and papers.
An engraving of Aparicio Saravia's general staff.
An old charcoal iron.
A clock stopped in time, with a broken pendulum.
A peeling gilt frame, with no canvas.
A cardboard chessboard, and some broken chessmen.
A stove with only two legs.
A chest made of leather.
A mildewed copy of Foxe's *Book of Martyrs,* in intricate
Gothic lettering.
A photograph which might be of anybody.
A worn skin, once a tiger's.
A key which has lost its lock.
What can we be looking for in the attic
except the flotsam of disorder?
To forgetting, to all forgotten objects, I have just erected
this monument
(unquestionably less durable than bronze) which will be
lost among them.

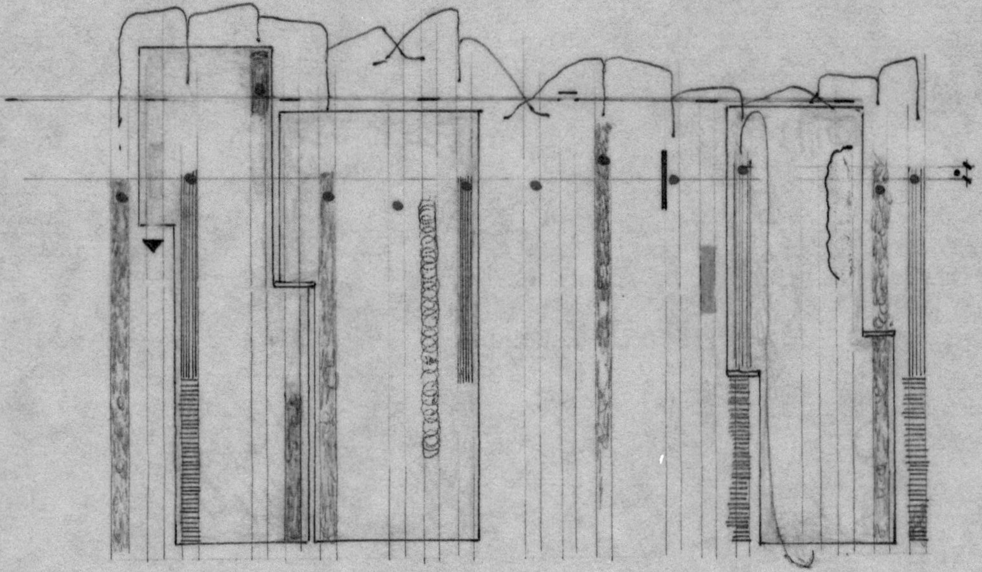

James Merrill "The World & the Child"

J Stone 2/2001

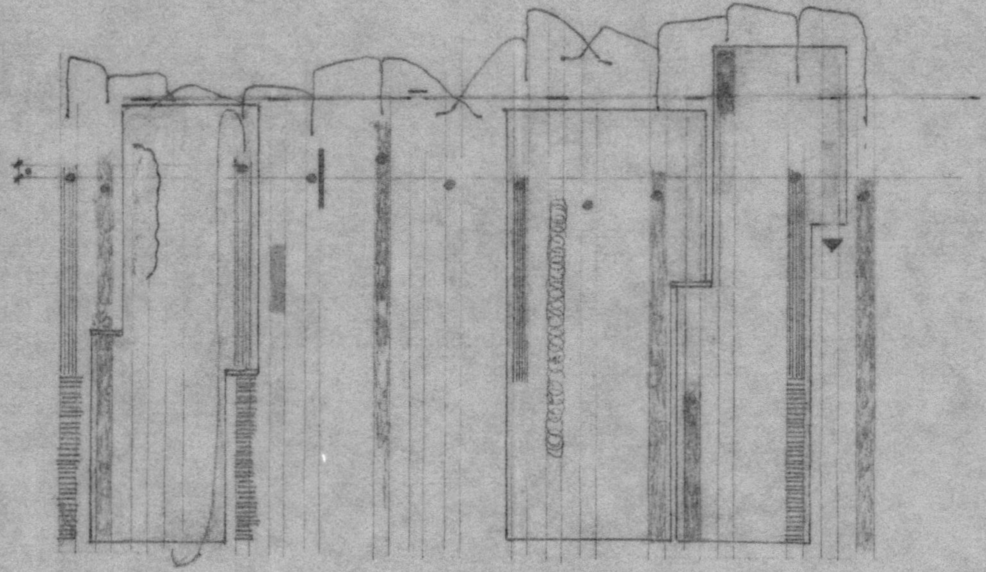

James Merrill "The World & the Child"

2/2001

James Merrill

THE WORLD AND THE CHILD

Letting his wisdom be the whole of love,
The father tiptoes out, backwards. A gleam
Falls on the child awake and wearied of,

Then, as the door clicks shut, is snuffed. The glove-
Gray afterglow appalls him. It would seem
That letting wisdom be the whole of love

Were pastime even for the bitter grove
Outside, whose owl's white hoot of disesteem
Falls on the child awake and wearied of.

He lies awake in pain, he does not move,
He will not call. The women, hearing him,
Would let their wisdom be the whole of love.

People have filled the room he lies above.
Their talk, mild variation, chilling theme,
Falls on the child. Awake and wearied of

Mere pain, mere wisdom also, he would have
All the world waking from its winter dream,
Letting its wisdom be. The whole of love
Falls on the child awake and wearied of.

Diana O'Hehir

HOUSE

Erased off the face of my earth, all that remains is a white space,
On it the possible ghost
Of roofline, window. I travel
Looking for myself in all the empty rooms
That say, why did you leave us.

Country of no-one. An open door, a dropped book, a photo of
me at the age of four.

I wait for myself on the stairs,
Touching a hand along the walls,
Move up behind myself, saying: Stop that.

In the upstairs room is the memory of another solitude; it once
Made a bright oxygen that raised my ribcage,
Touched against the insides of the windows, glowed out,
filled up the whole house

To roofline, timbers, where now my own ghost climbs,
And the sparrow swings in under the roof ridge
Her wings beating
Searching for something she's hidden there.

Diana O'Hehir

HOME

Somewhere there's a street of empty houses,
Roof after roof, the doors bleached white by memory

Which I, like the force of night, travel over,
Making stairs out of words, sounds too low to hear.

Again and again in dreams, I
Find the right house, open the door. All that vanished furniture
Unreproachful, calls itself by the right names.
And the stream still runs down the gully; the old woman, leathery
as a bat,
Is dabbling her yellow toes in it.
We lead her home slowly in her damp print dress,

While down at the end of the street God still lives.
Our children play a high white noise at late o'clock;
We call to them, out on the porches, under the leaf-knobbed trees:
Come here, come back,
But the houses are as transparent as Corinth,

The beautiful roofline folds up onto the sky
Closing us out.

Adrienne Rich

IN THE WAKE OF HOME

1. You sleep in a room with bluegreen curtains
posters   a pile of animals on the bed
A woman and a man who love you
and each other   slip the door ajar
you are almost asleep   they crouch in turn
to stroke your hair   you never wake
This happens every night for years.
This never happened.

2. Your lips   steady   never say
It should have been this way
That's not what you say
You   so carefully not asking, *Why?*
Your eyes   looking straight in mine
remind me of a woman's
auburn hair   my mother's hair
but you never saw that hair

The family coil   so twisted, tight and loose
anyone trying to leave
has to strafe the field
burn the premises down

3. The home houses
mirages   memory fogs the kitchen panes
the rush-hour traffic outside
has the same old ebb and flow
Out on the darkening block
somebody calls you home
night after night   then never again
Useless for you to know
they tried to do what they could
before they left for good

4. The voice that used to call you home
has gone off on the wind
beaten into thinnest air
whirling down other streets
or maybe the mouth was burnt to ash
maybe the tongue was torn out
brownlung has stolen the breath
or fear has stolen the breath
maybe under another name
it sings on AM radio:
And if you knew, what would you know?

5. But you will be drawn to places
where generations lie
side by side with each other:
fathers, mothers and children
in the family prayerbook
or the country burying-ground
You will hack your way back through the bush
to the *Jodensavanne*
where the gravestones are black with mould
You will stare at the old family albums
with their smiles their resemblances
you will want to believe that nobody
wandered off became strange
no woman dropped her baby and ran
no father took off for the hills
no axe splintered the door
—that once at least it was all in order
and nobody came to grief

6. Any time you go back
where absence began

the kitchen faucet sticks in a way you know
you have to pull the basement door
in before drawing the bolt
the last porch-step is still loose
the water from the tap
is the old drink of water
Any time you go back
the familiar underpulse
will start its throbbing: *Home, home!*
and the hole torn and patched over
will gape unseen again

7. Even where love has run thin
the child's soul musters strength
calling on dust-motes   song on the radio
closet-floor of galoshes
stray cat   piles of autumn leaves
whatever comes along
—the rush of purpose to make a life
worth living past abandonment
building the layers up again
over the torn hole   filling in

8. And what of the stern and faithful aunt
the fierce grandmother   the anxious sister
the good teacher   the one
who stood at the crossing when you had to cross
the woman hired to love you
the skeleton who held out a crust
the breaker of rules   the one
who is neither a man nor a woman
who warmed the liquid vein of life
and day after day whatever the need

handed it on to you?
You who did and had to do
so much for yourself   this was done for you
by someone who did what they could
when others left for good

9. You imagine an alley   a little kingdom
where the mother-tongue is spoken
a village of shelters   woven
or sewn of hides   in a long-ago way
a shanty standing up
at the edge of sharecropped fields
a tenement where life is seized by the teeth
a farm battened down on snowswept plains
a porch with rubber-plant and glider
on a steep city street
You imagine the people would all be there
fathers mothers and children
the ones you were promised would all be there
eating   arguing   working
trying to get on with life
you imagine this used to be
for everyone   everywhere

10. What if I told you your home
is this continent of the homeless
of children sold   taken by force
driven from their mother's land
killed by their mothers to save from capture
—this continent of changed names and mixed-up blood
of languages tabooed
diasporas unrecorded
undocumented refugees

underground railroads   trails of tears
What if I tell you your home
is this planet of warworn children
women and children standing in line or milling
endlessly calling each others' names
What if I tell you, you are not different
it's the family albums that lie
—will any of this comfort you
and how should this comfort you?

11. The child's soul carries on
in the wake of home
building a complicated house
a tree-house without a tree
finding places for everything
the song   the stray cat   the skeleton
The child's soul musters strength
where the holes were torn
but there are no miracles:
even children become exhausted
And how shall they comfort each other
who have come young to grief?
Who will number the grains of loss
and what would comfort be?

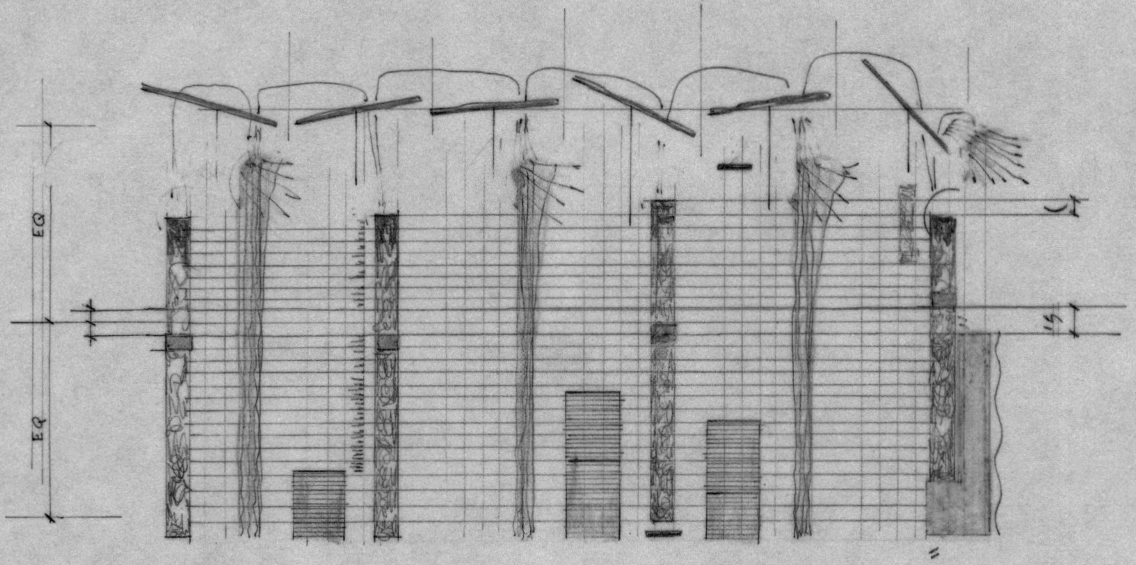

Jacqueline Osherow, "Villanelle for the Middle of the Night"   JStone 2/2001

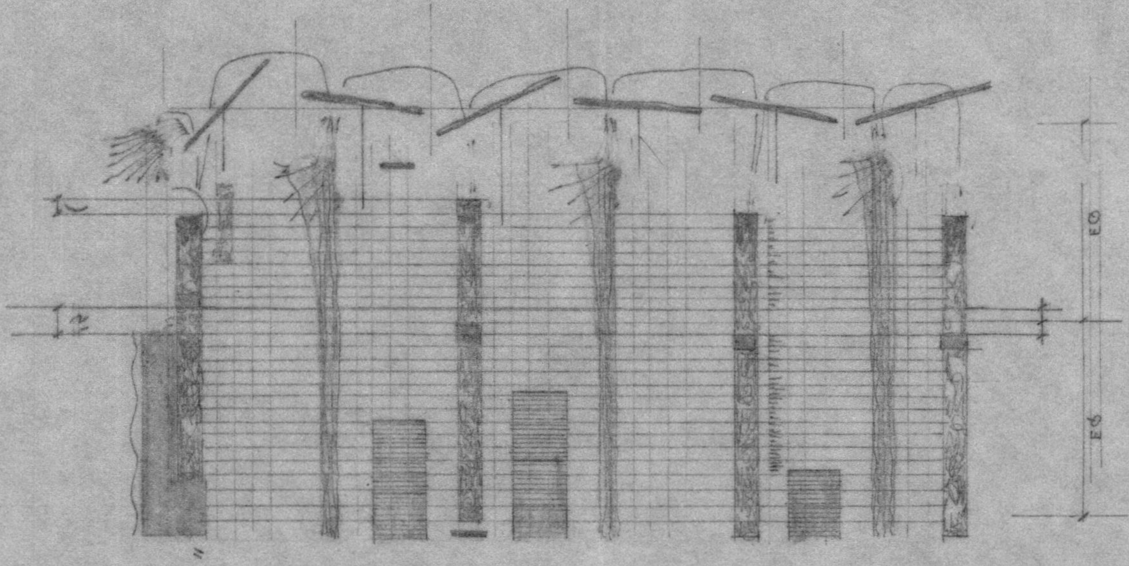

Jacqueline Osherow

VILLANELLE FOR THE MIDDLE OF THE NIGHT

Call it the refrigerator's hum at night,
The even breathing of a sleeping house
As a halo drifts in from a corner streetlight.

Awake, you train an ear to single out
A music jangling just beneath the noise.
Call it the refrigerator's hum at night.

Since you have no real hope of being accurate,
But what you mean is usually as diffuse
As a halo drifting from a corner streetlight.

Tonight, though, it is concentrated, intimate,
Luring you to store up what it says
(Call it the refrigerator's hum at night;

That, at least, accommodates the feel of it)
To try to temper yearning into praise,
As a halo drifting from a corner streetlight

Tempts an unsuspecting city street
With its otherworldly armory of shadows.
Call it the refrigerator hums at night.
Call it back. It's drifting mourns the streetlight.

Robert Frost

MENDING WALL

Something there is that doesn't love a wall,
That sends the frozen-ground-swell under it,
And spills the upper boulders in the sun;
And makes gaps even two can pass abreast.
The work of hunters is another thing:
I have come after them and made repair
Where they have left not one stone on a stone,
But they would have the rabbit out of hiding,
To please the yelping dogs. The gaps I mean,
No one has seen them made or heard them made,
But at spring mending-time we find them there.
I let my neighbor know beyond the hill;
And on a day we meet to walk the line
And set the wall between us once again.
We keep the wall between us as we go.
To each the boulders that have fallen to each.
And some are loaves and some are so nearly balls
We have to use a spell to make them balance:
"Stay where you are until our backs are turned!"
We wear our fingers rough with handling them.
Oh, just another kind of outdoor game,
One on a side. It comes to little more:
There where it is we do not need the wall:
He is all pine and I am apple orchard.
My apple trees will never get across
And eat the cones under his pines, I tell him.
He only says, "Good fences make good neighbors."
Spring is the mischief in me, and I wonder
If I could put a notion in his head:
"*Why* do they make good neighbors? Isn't it

Where there are cows? But here there are no cows.
Before I built a wall I'd ask to know
What I was walling in or walling out,
And to whom I was likely to give offense.
Something there is that doesn't love a wall,
That wants it down." I could say "Elves" to him,
But it's not elves exactly, and I'd rather
He said it for himself. I see him there
Bringing a stone grasped firmly by the top
In each hand, like an old-stone savage armed.
He moves in darkness as it seemed to me,
Not of woods only and the shade of trees.
He will not go behind his father's saying,
And he likes having thought of it so well
He says again, "Good fences make good neighbors."

John Updike

SUBURBAN MADRIGAL

Sitting here in my house,
looking through my windows
diagonally at my neighbor's house,
I see his sun-porch windows;
they are filled with blue-green,
the blue-green of my car,
which I parked in front of my house,
more or less, up the street,
where I can't directly see it.

How promiscuous is
the world of appearances!
How frail are property laws!
To him his window is filled with his
things: his lamps, his plants, his radio.
How annoyed he would be to know
that my car, legally parked,
yet violates his windows,
paints them full
(to me) of myself, my car,
my well-insured '55 Fordor Ford
a gorgeous green sunset streaking his panes.

Mark Strand

THE TUNNEL

A man has been standing
in front of my house
for days. I peek at him
from the living room
window and at night,
unable to sleep,
I shine my flashlight
down on the lawn.
He is always there.

After a while
I open the front door
just a crack and order
him out of my yard.
He narrows his eyes
and moans. I slam
the door and dash back
to the kitchen, then up
to the bedroom, then down.

I weep like a schoolgirl
and make obscene gestures
through the window. I
write large suicide notes
and place them so he
can read them easily.
I destroy the living
room furniture to prove
I own nothing of value.

When he seems unmoved
I decide to dig a tunnel
to a neighboring yard.
I seal the basement off
from the upstairs with
a brick wall. I dig hard
and in no time the tunnel
is done. Leaving my pick
and shovel below,

I come out in front of a house
and stand there too tired to
move or even speak, hoping
someone will help me.
I feel I'm being watched
and sometimes I hear
a man's voice,
but nothing is done
and I have been waiting for days.

Diana O'Hehir

THE OLD LADY UNDER THE FREEWAY

I've come down here to live on a bed of weeds.

Up there are white spaces with curving ceilings,
Harsh wide silver-fitted cars,
Marching squads of freckled-armed men.

My world is depths of green, a water of fern.
No one would guess that a safety hides here below,
Secretly jeweled, dropped in this special pocket.

I'm the mad old lady under the ledge. The good
Who fall headlong off the freeway bridge,
I salvage their nail files, pen knives;
I carve my way in with them;
I make a tunnel with green sides.

At night I lie on my back;
The ferns meet over my face like a lover's hair.
They nestle my ear. Their words are unsafe.
The words they say are harsh and green.

I'm roasting shreds of leaf, roasting soup in a can.
My air is as solid as the inside of a honeydew melon.

Rita Dove

GEOMETRY

I prove a theorem and the house expands:
the windows jerk free to hover near the ceiling,
the ceiling floats away with a sigh.

As the walls clear themselves of everything
but transparency, the scent of carnations
leaves with them. I am out in the open

and above the windows have hinged into butterflies,
sunlight glinting where they've intersected.
They are going to some point true and unproven.

CITY POEMS

The poet must be a subversive barbarian at the city gates, questioning reality and reinventing it.

Lawrence Ferlinghetti

WHAT IS A "CITY POEM"? The Indo-European root of the word *city* is *kei*, which means *to lie down*; the same root gives us such cozy nouns as *bed, beloved, dear,* and *home*. In the twentieth century both fiction and reality contradict this domestic image of the city as a place of 'lying down;'[28] so do many of the poems in this section. Prior to the mid-nineteenth century the city was either a destination for the traveling bard or the place the romantic poet left when heading for the lakes, not the subject of the poem itself.

Near the beginning of his epic 'autobiographical' poem *The Prelude*, William Wordsworth writes:

Whate'er its mission, the soft breeze can come
To none more grateful than to me; escaped
From the vast city, where I long had pined
A discontented sojourner: now free,
Free as a bird to settle where I will.[29]

For him the city's value is that it can be "escaped;" yet years earlier, one morning upon Westminster Bridge, he wrote (perhaps somewhat in spite of himself) these lines:

Earth has not anything to show more fair:
Dull would he be of soul who could pass by
A sight so touching in its majesty:
This City now doth, like a garment, wear
The beauty of the morning; silent, bare,
Ships, towers, domes, theatres, and temples lie
Open unto the fields, and to the sky.[30]

Wordsworth's flight from the "vast city" was typical of those in search of the sublime. Not until later in the nineteenth century did poetry discover, through the restless and melancholy spirit of Charles Baudelaire, aspects of the urban landscape that complement the pastoral beauty of lakes and fields with a darker beauty of shadows and crowds.

In a short prose piece titled "Crowds," Baudelaire writes: "It is not given to everyone to bathe in the multitude: to enjoy the crowd is an art,"[31] perhaps meaning that it is uniquely the art of the poet. Walter Benjamin devotes the largest section of his *Arcades Project*[32] to Baudelaire, representing him as the quintessential urban man who uses the constraints of the city to incite a passion for something else. Jean-Paul Sartre says of Baudelaire: "He wanted the earthly prison, so that he could feel that he was continually on the point of escaping it."[33] He had an aversion to both nature: "Vast woods, you terrify me like cathedrals"[34] and home: "A fairy has bestowed (upon me) the love of masks and masquerading, the hate of home and a passion for roaming."[35] Like Wordsworth he climbed a hill to look down on his city, but unlike the "theatres, domes and temples" of London, he sees below him a Paris dark with "brothel and hospital, prison, purgatory, hell."[36]

Baudelaire began his career by translating Poe's prose work into French.[37] One story in particular may have had a direct influence on the development of his concept of the *flâneur*.[38] In "The Man of the Crowd," Poe's narrator follows a figure for two days and two nights, through all the quarters of the city, determined to discover the man's destination, until he finally realizes that he has none. The mysterious figure is not *in* the crowd, but *of* the crowd; his very identity depends upon being surrounded by the multitudes. Thus he plunges into the crowded marketplace in the morning, and into the districts of disrepute late at night; always he goes where there are the most people, letting the urban rhythms of the day rebuild the edifice of bodies into which he perpetually disappears. Anonymity is clearly a prerequisite to being a man of the crowd. According to Baudelaire, it is also the prerogative of the urban poet: "The poet enjoys the incomparable privilege of being able to be himself or someone else, as he chooses...For him alone everything is vacant, and if certain places seem closed to him, it is only because in his eyes they are not worth visiting."[39]

Victor Hugo juxtaposes images of the crowded city and the untamed forest in these lines from "The Propensity from Reverie":

> Crowd without a name: Chaos!—voices, eyes, footsteps.
> Those never seen, never known.
> All the living!—cities buzzing in the ear
> More than any beehive of American woods.

He invokes the metaphor again when he writes that the poet "listens, by turns, to the forests and the crowd." These two potent images conjoin in Ezra Pound's "In A Station of the Metro," a poem whose nineteen syllables blend images of trees, weather, ghostliness, and human-kind into a vivid snapshot of the morning commute in the busy city. There are only two adjectives that fall in the second line of the poem—the *wet, black* bough; together they evoke a fecundity that contrasts with the evanescent "apparitions" of the first line.

"Here there used to be a bakery; there Madame Dupuis used to live."
Michel de Certeau, *The Practice of Everyday Life*

PROPER NAMES IN CITIES, like common objects at home, ground our experience in the familiar. Gregory Corso defines Paris as a "New Yorkless city"—it is *not* numbered streets forming an anonymous grid. Instead, it is a city defined by the names of its authors ("Artaud, Rimbaud, Appolinaire"), its neighborhoods

("Montparnassian woes"), and its history ("City of Germans dead and gone / Dollhouse of Mama War"). Osip Mandelstam's "Leningrad" is equally charged with the proper name. (In another poem, Mandelstam names a street after himself.)[40] Leningrad began as *St. Petersburg*, adopted its secular name in 1924 to honor the Soviet leader, and in 1930 when the poem was written the threat of "dear guests" at the door was part of the poet's daily life. In this last attempt to settle in the city of his birth, Mandelstam invokes the memory of the former "Petersburg" where he "has addresses still."

> *I think*
> *Of ancient cities of bringing to light*
> *Foundations under the foundations*
>
> Thom Gunn, "Bringing to Light"[41]

BOTH ABOVE GROUND AND BELOW, the city claims its own dreamlike vertical dimension that parallels Bachelard's narrative of the *oneiric* house. Thom Gunn must have been thinking primarily of Rome when he wrote "Bringing to Light" but in his poem "Diagrams" he invokes another dimension of the city—the weightless, indeterminate realm "where air ends and where steel begins." His "spectral points of stiffened net," recall these lines by Baudelaire:

> those prodigies of scaffolding 'round buildings under repair, applying their open-work architecture, so paradoxically beautiful, upon architecture's solid body.[42]

Gunn's construction workers bridge a century of American history; they "wear their yellow boots like moccasins," and his metaphor of an East Coast concrete slab as a "mesa of unfinished top" bridges three thousand miles of geography. In the next poem, Gunn introduces the beauty of the city's iron landscape—"no trellises, no vines," only scaffolding, fire escapes, and the Statue of Liberty in the distance. According to James Merrill, all of New York City is as temporary as scaffolding: "As usual in New York, everything is torn down / Before you have had time to care for it." Wandering the city after an illness, he is struck by the fact that that new buildings are as vulnerable as the old, that "the sickness of our time requires / That these as well be blasted in their prime. / You would think the simple fact of having lasted / threatened our cities like mysterious fires."[43]

Manhattan is hemmed in by water and can only spread upward, but cities like São Paulo and Los Angeles illustrate a more typical pathology of urban growth. An aerial view of São Paulo (now the third largest city on the globe) looks like a photomontage of the all the metropolises of the world, great clumps of buildings, each in itself the size of Chicago. Updike's L. A. propagates "new buildings in all mirror styles of blankness," while his São Paulo is grey and weighty, "no glass downtown shimmering / with peacock power, just the elephantine / color of poured concrete repeated in clusters." These two cities share the absence of center; both continue to grow at their edges "to a chaos but still open to the arrows / of Heaven."

Far under the traffic, deep in earth,
The unborn forest waits, still, for a thousand years.

Tomas Tranströmer, "Street Crossing"

BENEATH EVEN THE LAYERS OF BURIED CIVILIZATIONS, this "unborn forest" stands for all forms of nature that are waiting to reclaim the city. Pound's "wet, black bough" is an appropriate image to support the modern metaphor of the 'urban jungle,' as is Valéry's observation that the contemporary metropolis encourages primitive behavior: "The inhabitant of the great urban centers reverts to a state of savagery." Wendell Berry in "The Wild" makes a distinction between true nature and this urban wilderness: "In the empty lot—a place / not natural, but wild—among / the trash of human absence;" yet recent events suggest that the city is hospitable to a more literal nature as well. (The peregrine falcon, recently an endangered species in the American West, recovered from the brink of extinction when naturalists brought pairs of birds to the city to hatch their eggs.)[44] As nature has always been a subject for poetry, the language of poetry is ideally suited to explore this new urban vision.

Vast city (São Paulo), wild city (Los Angeles), erotic city (Venice), ruined city (Munich and Detroit)—all these cities-within-poems invite us to recognize the complex interrelationship of the global and the intimate, of the natural and the man-made. Walter Benjamin says of the *flâneur:* "The city splits for him into its dialectical poles. It opens up to him as a landscape, even as it closes around him like a room."[45] This dreamy juxtaposition of vast landscape and intimate room defines the mood of de Chirico's surrealistic paintings of Italian piazzas, two of which provide the context for Mark Strand's pair of villanelles in this section. In "The Philosopher's Conquest," Strand conspires with de Chirico to slow time to a virtual halt. "Why do the Clock hands say 1:28?" The train suggests noise and distance, yet shadows and objects are silent and near. In "The Disquieting Muses," "something about the silence of the square" confounds our preconditioned expectation for a lively urban space.

The line between surrealism and magical realism is not precise. Surrealism found its focus before the Second World War, and magical realism emerged after, but the urban context of his paintings places de Chirico in advance of his time. The context of magical realism is often the city: Calvino's visual fables of Venice,[46] Gabriel García Márquez's tropical Macondo,[47] Borges' infinite Library of Babel[48]—because such an alternative reality needs a large scope. In Diana O'Hehir's poem "The Retarded Children Find a World Built Just for Them," the dreamy magic of a García Márquez novel is compressed into twenty metered lines. This city confers upon "her jewels, the children" the freedom to "turn and turn like dancers," and the poem confers upon us, its readers, the freedom to imagine cities where "doors are ninety feet high."

"The delight of the urban poet is love—not at first sight but at last sight," writes Walter Benjamin;[49] he rightly suggests that loving cities takes time. Wordsworth's London wears "the beauty of the morning;" Robert Lowell's Paris is "coffined in its atmosphere." Each poet presents his city with reverence, and gives it human qualities. As we grow to love our cities, we move from visitor to *flâneur*. Remaining inconspicuous, we traverse the city horizontally and vertically, in subways and in elevators, in disappointment and in anticipation. Thus we return to Pound's metaphor—the Metro station as a branch, whose leaves are the faces of the crowd, of which our own is one. With these poems as guides, a city is reborn not as an impersonal accretion of mass, but as the setting of our own desire for space.

São Paulo, however vast, is still open to "the arrows / of Heaven," and likewise the canyons of New York demand our vertical gaze. Through the dust of demolition, and perhaps a bit visionary due to medication, James Merrill gives the architects of cities hope when he writes "back into my imagination / the city glides, like cities seen from the air."

Ezra Pound

IN A STATION OF THE METRO

The apparition of these faces in the crowd;
Petals on a wet, black bough.

Gregory Corso

PARIS

Childcity, Aprilcity,
Spirits of angels crouched in doorways,
Poets, worms in hair, beautiful Baudelaire,
Artaud, Rimbaud, Apollinaire,
Look to the nightcity—
Informers, concierges,
Montparnassian woe, deathical Notre Dame,
To the nightcircle look, dome heirloomed,
Hugo and Zola together entombed,
Harlequin deathtrap,
Seine generates ominous mud,
Eiffel looks down—sees the Apocalyptical ant crawl,
New Yorkless city,
City of Germans dead and gone,
Dollhouse of Mama War.

Osip Mandelstam, translated by *Bernard Meares*

LENINGRAD

I returned to my city, familiar as tears,
As veins, as mumps from childhood years.

You've returned here, so swallow as quick as you can
The cod-liver oil of Leningrad's riverside lamps.

Recognize when you can December's brief day:
Egg yolk folded into its ominous tar.

Petersburg, I don't yet want to die:
You have the numbers of my telephones.

Petersburg, I have addresses still
Where I can raise the voices of the dead.

I live on the backstairs and the doorbell buzz
Strikes me in the temple and tears at my flesh.

And all night long I await those dear guests of yours,
Rattling, like manacles, the chains on the doors.

Robert Lowell

BAUDELAIRE II. RECOLLECTION

Be calm, my Sorrow, you must move with care.
You asked for evening, it descends, it's here;
Paris is coffined in its atmosphere,
bringing some relief and others care.
Now while the common multitude strips bare,
feels pleasure's cat o'nine tails on its back,
accumulating remorse at the great bazaar—
give me your hand, my Sorrow. Let's stand back,
back from these people. Look, the defunct years, dressed
in period costume crowd the balconies of the sky.
Regret emerges smiling from the river,
the sun, worked overtime, sleeps beneath an arch...
and like a long shroud stretched from east to west—
listen, my Dearest, hear the sweet night march!

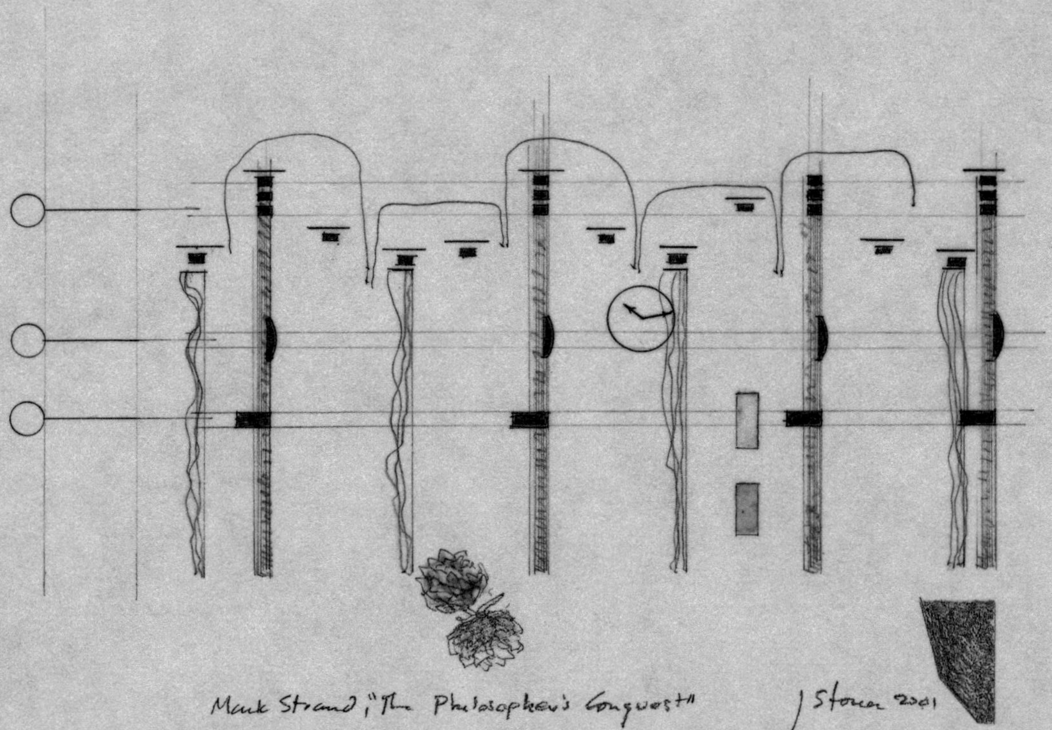

Mark Strand, "The Philosopher's Conquest"

J Stoner 2001

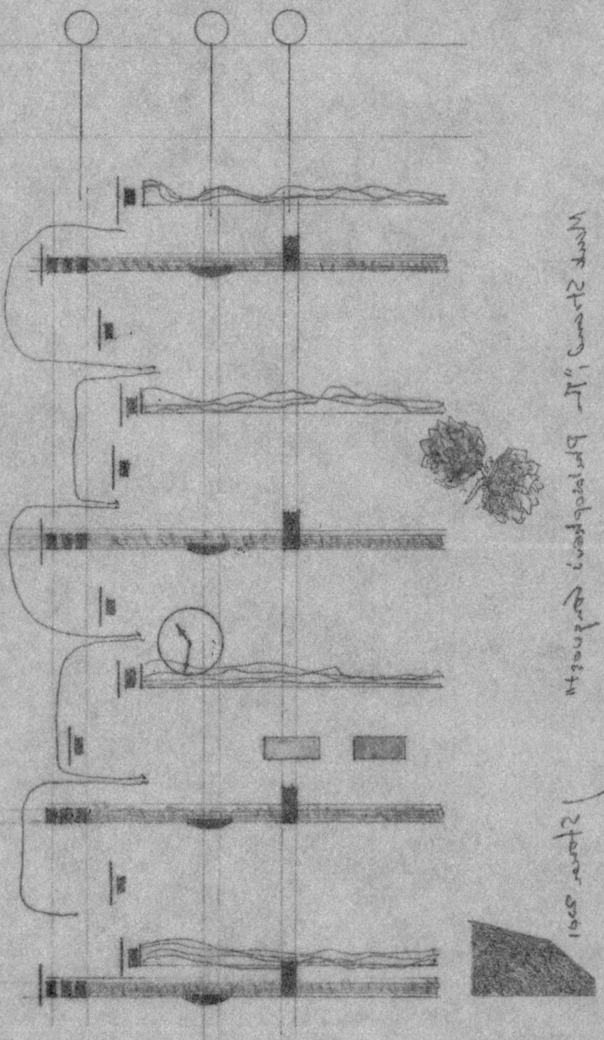

Mark Strand

THE PHILOSOPHER'S CONQUEST

This melancholy moment will remain,
So, too, the oracle beyond the gate,
And always the tower, the boat, the distant train.

Somewhere to the south a Duke is slain,
A war is won. Here, it is too late.
This melancholy moment will remain.

Here, an autumn evening without rain,
Two artichokes abandoned on a crate,
And always the tower, the boat, the distant train.

Is this another scene of childhood pain?
Why do the clockhands say 1:28?
This melancholy moment will remain.

The green and yellow light of love's domain
Falls upon the joylessness of fate,
And always the tower, the boat, the distant train.

The things our vision will us to contain,
The life of objects, their unbearable weight.
This melancholy moment will remain,
And always the tower, the boat, the distant train.

Thom Gunn

DIAGRAMS

Downtown, an office tower is going up.
And from the mesa of unfinished top
Big cranes jut, spectral points of stiffened net:
Angled top-heavy artefacts, and yet
Diagrams from the sky, as if its air
Could drop lines, snip them off, and leave them there.

On girders round them, Indians pad like cats,
With wrenches in their pockets and hard hats.

They wear their yellow boots like moccasins,
Balanced where air ends and where steel begins,
Sky men, and through the sole's flesh, chewed and pliant,
They feel the studded bone-edge of the giant.
It grunts and sways through its whole metal length.
And giving to the air is sign of strength.

Thom Gunn

IRON LANDSCAPES

(AND THE STATUE OF LIBERTY)

No trellisses, no vines
                                        a fire escape
Repeats a bare black Z from tier to tier.
Hard flower, tin scroll embellish this landscape.
Between iron columns I walk toward the pier.

And stand a long time at the end of it
Gazing at iron on the New Jersey side.
A girdered ferry-building opposite,
Displaying the name LACKAWANNA, seems to ride

The turbulent brown-grey waters that intervene:
Cool seething incompletion that I love.
The zigzags come and go, sheen tracking sheen;
And water wrestles with the air above.

But I'm at peace with the iron landscape too,
Hard because buildings must be hard to last
—Block, cylinder, cube, built with their angles true,
A dream of righteous permanence, from the past.

In Nixon's era, decades after the ferry,
The copper embodiment of the pieties
Seems hard, but hard like a revolutionary
With indignation, constant as she is.

From here you can glimpse her downstream, her far charm,
Liberty, tiny woman in the mist
—You cannot see the torch—raising her arm
Lorn, bold, as if saluting with her fist.

Barrow Street Pier, New York
May 1973

James Merrill

AN URBAN CONVALESCENCE

Out for a walk, after a week in bed,
I find them tearing up part of my block
And, chilled through, dazed and lonely, join the dozen
In meek attitudes, watching a huge crane
Fumble luxuriously in the filth of years.
Her jaws dribble rubble. An old man
Laughs and curses in her brain,
Bringing to mind the close of *The White Goddess*.

As usual in New York, everything is torn down
Before you have had time to care for it.
Head bowed, at the shrine of noise, let me try to recall
What building stood here. Was there a building at all?
I have lived on this same street for a decade.

Wait. Yes. Vaguely a presence rises
Some five floors high, of shabby stone
—Or am I confusing it with another one
In another part of town, or of the world?—
And over its lintel into focus vaguely
Misted with blood (my eyes are shut)
A single garland sways, stone fruit, stone leaves,
Which years of grit had etched until it thrust
Roots down, even into the poor soil of my seeing.
When did the garland become part of me?
I ask myself, amused almost,
Then shiver once from head to toe,

Transfixed by a particular cheap engraving of garlands
Bought for a few francs long ago,
All calligraphic tendril and cross-hatched rondure,
Ten years ago, and crumpled up to stanch
Boughs dripping, whose white gestures filled a cab,

And thought of neither then nor since.
Also, to clasp them, the small, red-nailed hand
Of no one I can place. Wait. No. Her name, her features
Lie toppled underneath that year's fashions.
The words she must have spoken, setting her face
To fluttering like a veil, I cannot hear now,
Let alone understand.

So that I am already on the stair,
As it were, of where I lived,
When the whole structure shudders at my tread
And soundlessly collapses, filling
The air with motes of stone.
Onto the still erect building next door
Are pressed levels and hues—
Pocked rose, streaked greens, brown whites.
Who drained the pousse-café?
Wires and pipes, snapped off at roots, quiver.

Well, that is what life does. I stare
A moment longer, so. And presently
The massive volume of the world
Closes again.

Upon that book I swear
To abide by what it teaches:
Gospels of ugliness and waste,
Of towering voids, of soiled gusts,
Of a shrieking to be faced
Full into, eyes astream with cold—

With cold?
All right then. With self-knowledge.

Indoors at last, the pages of *Time* are apt
To open, and the illustrated mayor of New York,
Given a glimpse of how and where I work,
To note yet one more house that can be scrapped.

Unwillingly I picture
My walls weathering in the general view.
It is not even as though the new
Buildings did very much for architecture.
Suppose they did. The sickness of our time requires
That these as well be blasted in their prime.
You would think the simple fact of having lasted
Threatened our cities like mysterious fires.

There are certain phrases which to use in a poem
Is like rubbing silver with quicksilver. Bright
But facile, the glamour deadens overnight.
For instance, how "the sickness of our time"

Enhances, then debases, what I feel.
At my desk I swallow in a glass of water
No longer cordial, scarcely wet, a pill
They had told me not to take until much later.

With the result that back into my imagination
The city glides, like cities seen from the air,
Mere smoke and sparkle to the passenger
Having in mind another destination

Which now is not that honey-slow descent
Of the Champs-Elysées, her hand in his,
But the dull need to make some kind of house
Out of the life lived, out of the love spent.

John Updike

SÃO PAULO

Buildings to the horizon, an accretion
big beyond structure: no glass downtown shimmering
with peacock power, just the elephantine
color of poured concrete repeated in clusters,
into the haze that foots the horizon of hills,
a human muchness encountering no bounds.

From the hotel window, ridged roofs of ruddy tile,
the black of corrugated iron, the green
and yellow of shopfronts, a triangular hut
revealed survival's piecemeal, patchwork logic.
All afternoon, the view sulked beneath my room
in silence—a city without a city's outcry.

And then a pronouncement—thunder?—overruled
the air conditioner's steady whir, and a tapping
asked me to *look*. The empty, too-full view
held thousands of foreshortened arrows: rain,
seen from above, a raying angelic substance.
I felt lifted up, to God's altitude.

If the rain was angelic, why not men and their works?
Their colorless habitations, like a drenched
honeycomb: men come in from the country
to the town's crowded hope, the town grown
to a chaos but still open to the arrows
of Heaven, transparently, all life a veil.

John Updike

L. A.

Lo, at its center one can find oneself
atop a paved and windy hill, with weeds
taller than men on one side and on the other
a freeway thundering a canyon's depth below.
New buildings in all mirror-styles of blankness
are being assembled by darkish people while
the old-time business blocks that Harold Lloyd
teetered upon crouch low, in shade, turned slum.

The lone pedestrian stares, scooped at by space.
the palms are isolate, like psychopaths.
Conquistadorial fevers reminisce
in the adobe band of smog across the sky,
its bell of blue a promise that lured too many
to this waste of angels, of ever-widening gaps.

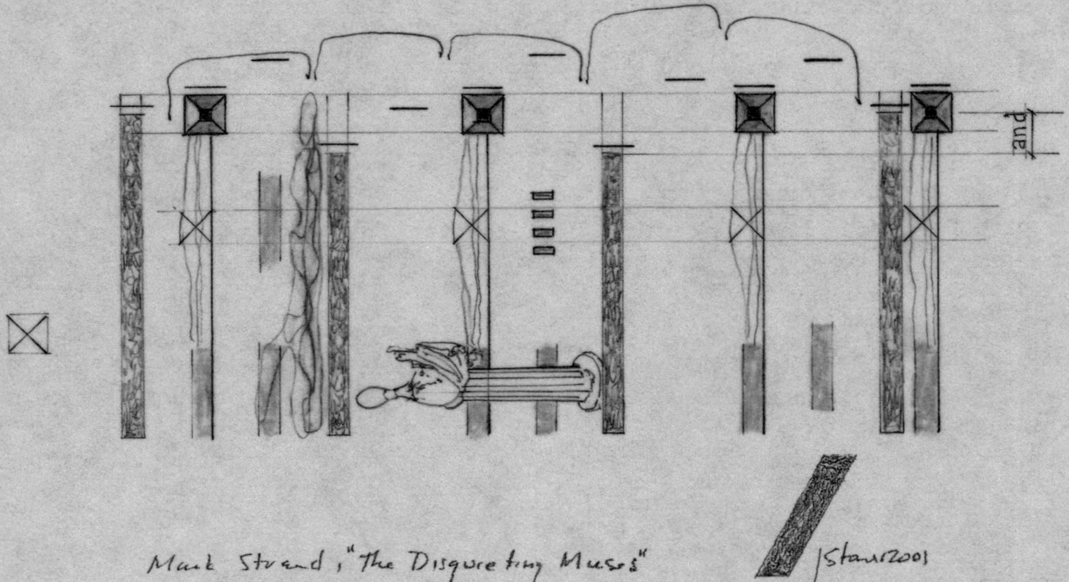

Mark Strand, "The Disquieting Muses"

JStarr2001

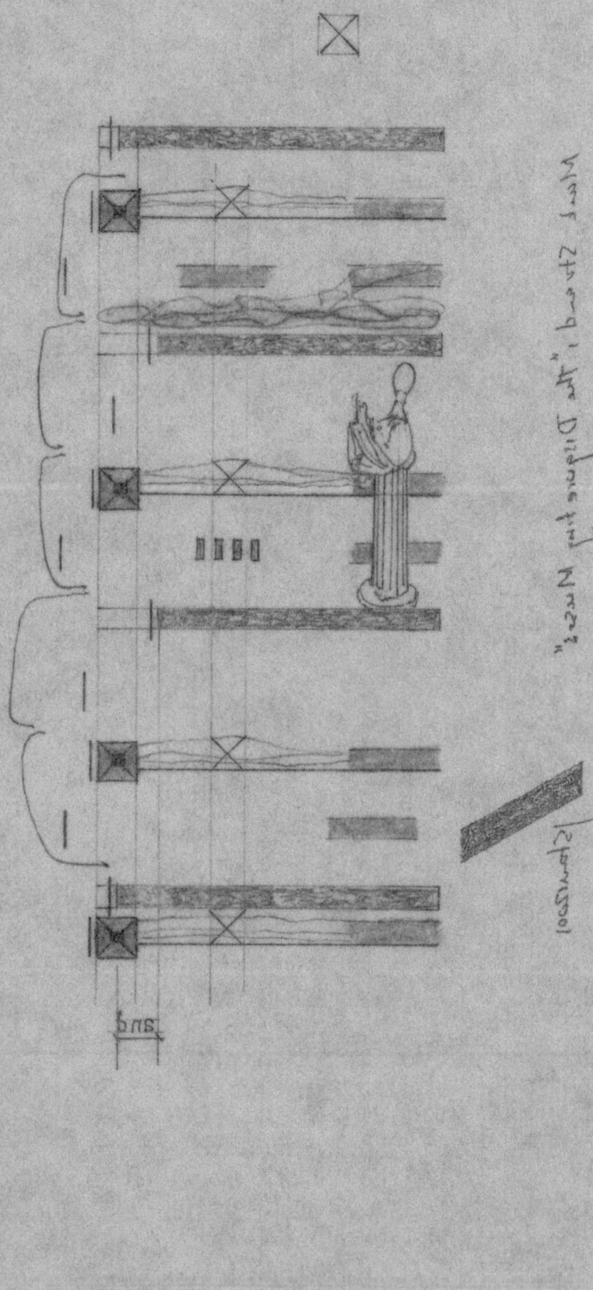

Mark Strand

THE DISQUIETING MUSES

Boredom sets in first, and then despair.
One tries to brush it off. It only grows.
Something about the silence of the square.

Something is wrong; something about the air,
Its color; about the light, the way it glows.
Boredom sets in first, and then despair.

The muses in their fluted evening wear,
Their faces blank, might lead one to suppose
Something about the silence of the square,

Something about the buildings standing there.
But no, they have no purpose but to pose.
Boredom sets in first, and then despair.

What happens after that, one doesn't care.
What brought one here—the desire to compose
Something about the silence of the square,

Or something else, of which one's not aware,
Life itself, perhaps—who really knows?
Boredom sets in first, and then despair...
Something about the silence of the square.

Susan Mitchell

VENICE

Furtive, that's the version I want.
With eyes averted. Downcast, a little sly.
It's where it's looking, that's
where I want us—
in a harbor where we in our gondola
stare up and up at the enormous
freighters rusting the Adriatic, the ocean
oiled and ropy, scary even,
the way the waters seem higher than
our boat, about to topple onto.
Did I forget to say it's night, we're
seeing by artificial light how thin
flakes of snow are falling from. So easy
to say *the sky*, but that
would be wrong. We could puzzle over
how to say this. Or we could kiss.
Let's kiss, standing up in
scary, its huge hood lowering,
cover of darkness down
which the Crusaders with lances and crosses
high held in a once-upon-a-time still
tarnishing, still audible version
of a version of a version.
There's a vertigo to history different
from the vertigo of sex.
The children sold into slavery, into brothels.
The sores. The futility of crying and the futility
of stories that gradually wash up
on other shores. To what purpose all this
telling, version by version

deteriorating like silk, the patterns
no longer recognizable: ripple by ripple, the lush
lappings as if certain words, *pietá*
or *sofferenza*, were enough.
I had wanted to sightsee, to be taken slowly
by gondola, canal by canal, where Byron,
where shadows on stilts or like inverted
bells somberly under the arches
swaying, and Goethe, who stood on the foamy
crescendos and saw the *chiaro*
nell'chiaro and bibelots
of old and charming, the glimmers
well worn where the moon
all its chandeliers and stairways let down
into the sea-black sea. To stand
on the outstretched lip of
what might be called a romantic evening,
though already that version is
starting to bore me. It's not a question
of what's true or not true, it's more
a matter of what I want to hear.
Which is why we are standing in a boat
perilously small and stiffening
our necks to size the hugeness
of prows—barnacle-studded, ironclad, steely
beaked, with involucral bracts, with
scale on scale, a rust of buds.
Yes, that's how I want us, our love
pressed mouth to mouth
with history, and if with a partition,

then something thin
as lingerie.
I don't want us anesthetized, I want
us terrified and tied to it.
I used to think *it* was teeming, alive
with voices, flashings, with
music in which the dark lit candles.
I tried to reach any way
I could, rung by rung
or with sex shouldering me all the way.
Well, now I think otherwise.
More of a wall or impasse, more of—nothing.
Which isn't to say I'm not moved.
What tumbles through is icy and swift
and doesn't stop. I want us pressed
to that when you shove into me.
No candles. Not even darkness.

Tadeusz Borowski translated by *Tadeusz Pióro*

A WALK THROUGH MUNICH*

still life:

I walk through the city
apartment buildings,
government offices
built of marble,
sheathed in basalt,
which we tore out of cliffs
in Flossenburg, Mattausen, Lissa...
I look, I think: gasoline,
some hand grenades
a work detail,
and so, house after house
street after street,
quarter after quarter
one city after another,
like the ghetto in Warsaw;
as if this were a beautiful work of architecture:
above—the clear sky,
below—the burnt-out walls

**This is a long poem of many sections, separately titled, of which "still life" is one.*

Jill Stoner

FARMING DETROIT

Not of the lust for land or mines of gold,
That war gave birth to dreams from inside out.
They landed on the fragile shores of hope
And left a quarter hundred years in doubt.
Amidst the rubble ruins beat the rains
To weep a prayer of green upon the blight.
The weeds that fairly quilt the city plains
Now cast their wilderness to distant sight.

Yet 'neath black bricks the fertile earth lies still
In sleep, not death. It only asks now we
Should clear the mind of rage, the acres till
With cultivating hearts; sow patiently.
Or simply birds, by passing overhead
Will plant fruit trees in devastation's stead.

Northwest Airlines: Detroit–San Francisco, March 1990

Wendell Berry

THE WILD

In the empty lot—a place
not natural, but wild—among
the trash of human absence,

the slough and shamble
of the city's seasons, a few
old locusts bloom.

A few woods birds
fly and sing
in the new foliage

—warblers and tanagers, birds
wild as leaves; in a million
each one would be rare,

new to the eyes. A man
couldn't make a habit
of such color,

such flight and singing.
But they're the habit of this
wasted place. In them

the ground is wise. They are
Its remembrance of what it is.

Diana O'Hehir

THE RETARDED CHILDREN FIND A WORLD BUILT JUST FOR THEM

The doors of that city are ninety feet high,
On their panels are frescoes of ships, of mountains.

Inside is the children's kingdom
Where the mad ones, the foot-draggers, garglers,

Askew as a tower of beads,
Are sustained by the air. Buildings, like great gold chains

Emboss themselves around
The crazy children, their jewels.

The children turn and turn like dancers,
Their sweaters whirl out at their waists, their long chopped hair

Scrapes the sides of the archways,
They're happy, they're famous.

They walk on the streets in crystal shoes, lapis flows in the gutters;
Around the edge of each building there's a scarlet halo.

And those children with eyes like scars, with tongues sewed to the
roof of their palates, with hands that jerk

Like broken-backed squirrels,
Feed the writing of light from the buildings;

They forgive us ninety times over;
They sing and sing like all the birds of the desert.

INTERLUDE:

THE JAR & THE FIELD

Words move, music moves
Only in time; but that which is only living
Can only die. Words, after speech, reach
Into the silence. Only by the form, the pattern,
Can words or music reach
The stillness, as a Chinese jar still
Moves perpetually in its stillness.

T. S. Eliot, "Burnt Norton," *Four Quartets*

Un coup de dés n'abolira jamais le hazard.[50]

Stephane Mallarmé, "Un Coup de Dés"

BETWEEN THE STUDY OF POETRY AND THE STUDY OF ARCHITECTURE I spent a year living and working at sea, a year during which the interior I inhabited alternated between the smallest cabin below deck and the widest room whose walls and ceiling were the horizon and the starry sky. Aboard a small boat in the middle of the Atlantic Ocean (presumably as far from the constructed world as one could get) I fell in love with an idea of architecture that had nothing to do with buildings. On that equivocal watery landscape, which was sometimes as flat as Kansas and at others as hilly as Wales, with no landfall for six weeks, I and my six shipmates were inside a different kind of space—a kind for which there is no corresponding outside. It was then that I became convinced that all space is an interior.

ELIOT'S CHINESE JAR falls somewhere along the twentieth century trajectory that begins with a classic structure of hierarchy and center, and ends with a spatial algebra both abstract and pure. All but the first poem in this section evince the concept of relativity—just as Einstein gave poetic license to science, so do these poets give us the license to break the so-called 'rules' of architecture. They provoke us to question our prevailing assumptions that the axis is desirable, that the map is legible, and that the forest is impenetrable. Poetry is an art of risk, and these poems challenge architects to chart our new course without a compass.

In Tomas Tranströmer's prose poem, the forest harbors a mysterious clearing "which can only be found by those that have gotten lost." Baudelaire 'lost' himself in the streets of Paris for the purpose of remaining anonymous; in Tranströmer's forest one gets lost in order to find oneself. Elizabeth Bishop's "One Art" praises "the art of losing" not self, but objects; she strips value from things and hands it instead to experience. Her poem questions the worth of both substance and permanence, two of the characteristics of that which has traditionally deserved the name of architecture. The poems that follow expand upon this temporal relativity; through "ponderous deflations of distance" and "signals of enigma," the drifting curtains of Wallace Stevens and Eavan Boland develop abstractions of time through movement and through pattern.

Work stops at sunset. Darkness falls over the building site. The sky is filled with stars. "There is the blueprint," they say.

Italo Calvino, *Invisible Cities*

STARS MAP OUR WAY TO LANDFALL when we triangulate our position relative to them—essentially, we become part of a mobile map. But Mark Strand's black maps have no coordinates; even the stars are extinguished. Black is the color of the unknown, a condition that many of the poems in this section celebrate. Through images of stone and shadow, of weight and weightlessness they transform such ordinary notions as the thickness of a line and the location of a middle into metaphysical speculations. "Anecdote of the Jar" celebrates hierarchy; the poems that follow move relentlessly from this ordered power of an object toward the abstract diagram of a field.

In an essay titled "Field," John Berger contemplates a meadow that he sees every day, but has never really paid attention to. His musings conclude:

> At first I referred to the field as a space awaiting events; now I refer to it as an event in itself. But this inconsistency parallels exactly the apparently illogical nature of the experience. Suddenly an experience of disinterested observation opens in its center and gives birth to a happiness which is instantly recognizable as your own.
>
> The field you are standing before appears to have the same proportions as your own life.[51]

To live inside one's life is to work subjectively; this perhaps comes more naturally to poets than to architects. Berger describes an experience that can only be called an epiphany. When "the field awaiting events" became "the event in itself," it opened up to make room for him; he was no longer just observing, but neither was he in control. He became a player in a play which he therefore could no longer direct.

Listen to how the first person in this sequence of poems moves from active to passive voice, from verbs of action to verbs of being: "I place a jar in Tennessee" (Stevens), "I fix a line" (Rich), "I'm not at the bottom, I'm not at the top" (Milne), "I'd rather be horizontal" (Plath), "I am back in the communications net" (Tranströmer), and finally, "I am what is missing" (Strand). This abdication challenges the traditionally anthropocentric mission of the architect's profession; thus these poems may give us pause.

"In a field I am the absence of field," begins the final poem of this sequence, Strand's "Keeping Things Whole." The "I" claims identity not through presence but through absence; his universe is held together not by geometry but by motion. Like Poe's man of the crowd, the narrator of this remarkably spatial and temporal poem has no destination. He is, as Paul Klee writes in the first section of his *Pedagogical Sketchbook,*[52] "an *active* line on a walk, moving freely, without goal." His 'field' is that invisible landscape that parallels the visible one in which we go to work, come home, go to the store. "Keeping Things Whole" suggests a map like the worn paths through public parks, where innumerable traces tell a story that can never be fully deciphered.

After Klee, "Two secondary lines, moving around an imaginary main line."

The word *field* comes from a root that means *flat, to spread*. Yet in the twentieth century *field* became a partner to *force,* a function of time as much as of space. When the contents of that jar in Tennessee are emptied, they create a force of their own, and enclose us in a temporal flux that defies the clairvoyant arrogance of a 'ten year master plan.' In time as well as in space, our condition of being 'inside' the field of operation is absolute.

IN 1989, I received a fellowship to travel to Germany to make a theoretical study of the spatial condition at the Berlin Wall. In November the political wall came down, and when I arrived with my son in December we armed ourselves with hammer and chisel to join the crowds who were enthusiastically bringing down the physical wall as well. At this point the wall was composed of a pattern of holes though which people from both sides reached to touch hands. This vestigial membrane with its poignant 'windows' expressed a unity that was absent when I returned six months later. In June of 1990, all that marked the line of the wall were merchants selling chunks of concrete that looked suspiciously neutral. It was then that I remembered something I had read years before—a West German minister saying, "The wall is perhaps the only thing holding the two Germanys together."

Days later, on a crowded night train from Berlin to Warsaw, I played chess with a young Polish man from Posnan. Because he was extremely tired, he fell asleep after each move; nevertheless, he won the game. When I asked about his strategy, he explained that for him each move is an event, that when a Pole plays chess, he is reenacting the history of his country in miniature. He occupies a field of action whose boundaries are fluid, and which has no center. He does not plan; he merely reacts.

This kind of defensive strategy is what I propose for the architects of the twenty-first century—plan less, but react more aggressively; be flexible, and relinquish control. Accept the position of being *within* a space even while you are designing it. Explore a more equivocal concept of boundary, delight in the ambiguity of a wall that joins two spaces together. Play an endless game on the fine-grained board of the contemporary metropolis, where the center disappears as soon as you arrive there because it is really not a center at all, where every move will always engender another and because of this, the 'project' can never be finished.

"Poetry," writes John Berger, "can repair no loss, but it defies the space which separates...by its continual labor of reassembling what has been scattered."[53] Sometimes scattered, sometimes torn; like the poet, the architect is a tailor moving loosely through the landscape, sewing together seams that will always continue to come apart.

Wallace Stevens

ANECDOTE OF THE JAR

I placed a jar in Tennessee
And round it was, upon a hill.
It made the slovenly wilderness
Surround that hill.

The wilderness rose up to it,
And sprawled around, no longer wild.
The jar was round upon the ground
And tall and of a port in air.

It took dominion everywhere.
The jar was gray and bare.
It did not give of bird or bush
Like nothing else in Tennessee.

Adrienne Rich

BOUNDARY

What has happened here will do
To bite the living world in two,
Half for me and half for you.
Here at last I fix a line
Severing the world's design
Too small to hold both yours and mine.
There's enormity in a hair
Enough to lead men not to share
Narrow confines of a sphere
But put an ocean or a fence
Between two opposite intents.
A hair would span the difference.

A. A. Milne

HALFWAY DOWN

Halfway down the stairs
Is a stair
Where I sit.
There isn't any
Other stair
Quite like
It.
I'm not at the bottom,
I'm not at the top;
So this is the stair
Where
I always
Stop.

Halfway up the stairs
Isn't up,
And isn't down.
It isn't in the nursery
It isn't in the town.
And all sorts of funny thoughts
Run round my head:
"It isn't really
Anywhere!
It's somewhere else
Instead!"

Sylvia Plath

I AM VERTICAL

But I would rather be horizontal.
I am not a tree with my root in the soil
Sucking up minerals and motherly love
So that each March I may gleam into leaf,
Nor am I the beauty of a garden bed
Attracting my share of Ahs and spectacularly painted,
Unknowing I must soon unpetal.
Compared with me, a tree is immortal
And a flower-head not tall, but more startling,
And I want the one's longevity and the other's daring.

Tonight, in the infinitesimal light of the stars,
The trees and flowers have been strewing their cool odors.
I walk among them, but none of them are noticing.
Sometimes I think that when I am sleeping
I must most perfectly resemble them—
Thoughts gone dim.
It is more natural to me, lying down.
Then the sky and I are in open conversation,
And I shall be useful when I lie down finally:
Then the trees may touch me for once, and the flowers have
time for me.

I AM VERTICAL

Michael Ondaatje

THE FIRST RULE OF SINHALESE ARCHITECTURE

Never build three doors
in a straight line

A devil might rush
through them
deep into your house,
into your life

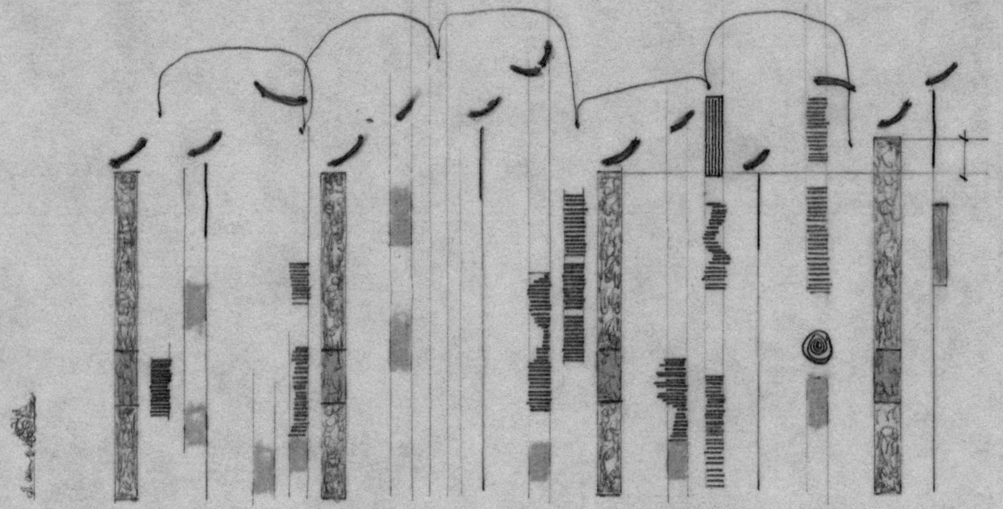

Elizabeth Bishop - "One Art"

J Stoner 2001

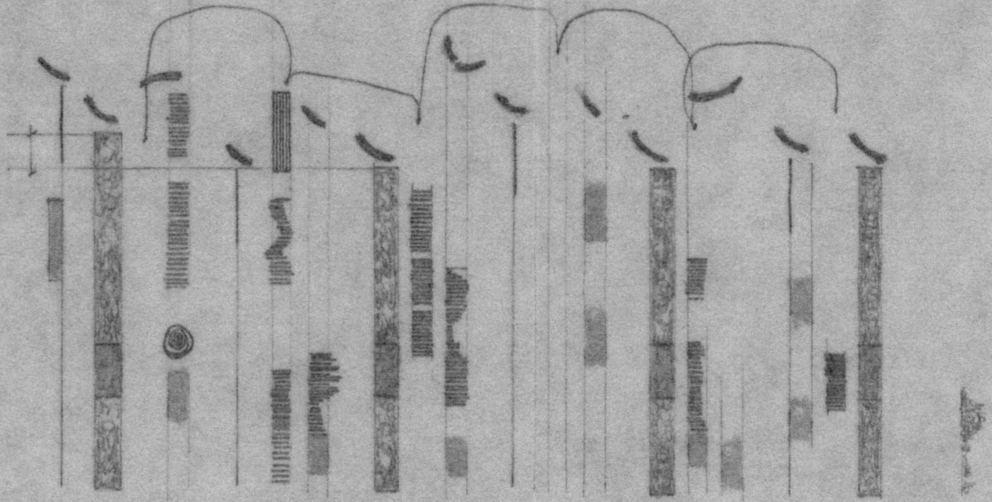

Elizabeth Bishop - "One Art"

J Stoner 2001

Elizabeth Bishop

ONE ART

The art of losing isn't hard to master;
so many things seem filled with the intent
to be lost that their loss is no disaster.

Lose something every day. Accept the fluster
of lost door keys, the hour badly spent.
The art of losing isn't hard to master.

Then practice losing farther, losing faster:
places, and names and where it was you meant
to travel. None of these will bring disaster.

I lost my mother's watch. And look! my last, or
next-to-last, of three loved houses went.
The art of losing isn't hard to master.

I lost two cities, lovely ones. And, vaster,
some realms I owned, two rivers, a continent
I miss them, but it wasn't a disaster.

—Even losing you (the joking voice, a gesture
I love) I shan't have lied. It's evident
the art of losing's not too hard to master
though it may look like (*Write* it!) like disaster.

Robert Creeley

AFTER MALLARMÉ

Stone,
like stillness,
around you my
mind sits, it is

a proper form
for
it, like
stone, like

compression itself,
fixed fast,
grey,
without a sound.

Wallace Stevens

THE CURTAINS IN THE HOUSE OF THE METAPHYSICIAN

It comes about that the drifting of these curtains
Is full of long motions; as the ponderous
Deflations of distance; or as clouds
Inseparable from their afternoons;
Or the changing of light, the dropping
Of the silence, wide sleep and solitude
Of night, in which all motion
Is beyond us, as the firmament,
Up-rising and down-falling, bares
The last largeness, bold to see.

Eavan Boland

HANGING CURTAINS WITH AN ABSTRACT PATTERN IN A CHILD'S ROOM

I chose these for you—
not the precinct of the unicorn, nor

the half-torn
singlet of a nursery rhyme prince, but

the signals of enigma:
Ellipse. Triangle. A music of ratio.

Draw these lines
against a winter dusk. Let them stand in for

frost on the spider's web and on
bicycle sheds.

Observe
how the season enters pure line

like a soul: all the signs we know
are only ways

of coming to our senses.
I can see

the distances off-loading color now
into angles as

I hang their weather in
your room, all the time wondering

just how I look from the road—
my blouse off-white and

my skirt the color of
all the disappointments of a day when

the curtains are pulled back on
a dull morning.

Mark Strand

BLACK MAPS

Not the attendance of stones,
nor the applauding wind,
shall let you know
you have arrived,

nor the sea that celebrates
only departures,
nor the mountains,
nor the dying cities.

Nothing will tell you
where you are.
Each moment is a place
you've never been.

You can walk
believing you cast
a light around you.
But how will you know?

The present is always dark.
Its maps are black,
rising from nothing,
describing,

in their slow ascent
into themselves,
their own voyage,
its emptiness,

the bleak, temperate
necessity of its completion.
As they rise into being
they are like breath.

And if they are studied at all
it is only to find,
too late, what you thought
were concerns of yours

do not exist.
Your house is not marked
on any of them,
nor are your friends,

waiting for you to appear,
nor are your enemies,
listing your faults.
Only you are there,

saying hello
to what you will be,
and the black grass
is holding up the black stars.

Tomas Tranströmer, translated by *Robert Bly*

THE CLEARING

In the middle of the forest there's an unexpected clearing which can only be found by those who have gotten lost.

The clearing is surrounded by a forest that is choking itself. Black trunks with the lichen's bristly beard. The jammed trees are dead all the way to the top, there a few solitary green branches touch the light. Underneath: shadows sitting on shadows, the marsh increasing.

But in the clearing the grass is curiously green and alive. Big stones lie around as if placed that way. They must have been foundation stones for a house, maybe I'm wrong. Who lived there? No one can help with that. The name sleeps somewhere in the archive no one opens (only archives remain young). The oral tradition is dead, and with it the memories. The gypsy tribe remembers, but those who can write forget. Write it down and forget it.

This little house hums with voices. It is the center of the world. But the people in it die or move away. This history ends. The place stands empty year after year. And the crofter's house becomes a sphinx. At the end everything has gone away except the foundation stones.

I've been here before somehow, but it's time to leave. I dive in among the briary underbrush. To get through it you have to take one step forward and two steps to the side, like a chess piece. Slowly it thins out and the light increases. My steps grow longer. A path wiggles its way toward me. I am back in the communications net.

On the humming high voltage pole a beetle sits in the sun. Under his gleaming shoulders his flight wings are lying, folded as ingeniously as a parachute packed by an expert.

Mark Strand

KEEPING THINGS WHOLE

In a field
I am the absence
of field.
This is
always the case.
Wherever I am
I am what is missing.

When I walk
I part the air
and always
the air moves in
to fill the spaces
where my body's been.

We all have reasons
for moving.
I move
to keep things whole.

SIX VILLANELLES

& OTHER THOUGHTS ON DRAWING FROM POEMS

Poetry is governed by the two-fold principle of "variety within unity."
Octavio Paz, *The Other Voice*

The regulating line is a means to an end; it is not a recipe.
Le Corbusier, *Toward a New Architecture*

WRAP A PHENOMENON IN WORDS, in layers of repeating lines in an order that suggests two distinct voices, assure that it has no real beginning or end. Further shape these words into a structure of six stanzas, the first five of three lines each, the last of four. The final lines of the first and second stanzas must rhyme, and then repeat alternately as the final lines of stanzas three, four, and five. These two lines appear once more as a heroic couplet at the end of the final stanza. This is the specification for a villanelle.

One may perhaps think of this kind of poetic form as the equivalent of building typology in architecture. Banister Fletcher's *History of Architecture According to the Comparative Method*[54] is organized according to typologies of such buildings as Greek temples, medieval timber churches, and Gothic cathedrals; more recently, cultural historians have illustrated and discussed the subtle variations within such vernacular typologies as African villages, roadside diners, and Irish rural houses.[55] Now, the simple volumes[56] of modern building types such as the 'high-rise' office and the 'big box' retail offer to architecture new 'closed form' typologies for experimentation. My premise is that the study of closed forms in the art of poetry can help us to understand the potential for the art of modern architecture to rewrite itself. This new architectural canon, distributed across time instead of geography, can equally well demonstrate the "variety within unity" of which Paz speaks.

Four primary devices define closed form in poetry: rhyme, meter, repetition and stanza. Not all closed forms use all of these—the sonnet does not customarily include repetition, and the end-words in the lines of the sestina do not rhyme. Blank verse employs neither repetition nor rhyme, only meter; the villanelle makes use of all four. Inquiry into the architectural analogues for each of these devices leads us to ever more metaphysical questions, like: "How can architecture rhyme?"

Rhyme belongs to the dazzling couplets of arrival.

Robert Hass, "Not Going to New York: A Letter"

RHYME AND METER represent respectively the vertical and horizontal systems of classic structure in poetry. Like columns and beams, they depend upon one another; like columns and beams also, in the best poems they remain so intrinsic to the structure that they forebear to overwhelm the sense of the whole with their details; they are nearly invisible.

Rhyme, normally a device that marks the ends of lines, forms a porous edge at the right margin of the poem. In architecture we can look to edge conditions like sidewalks and waterfronts for their rhyming potential:

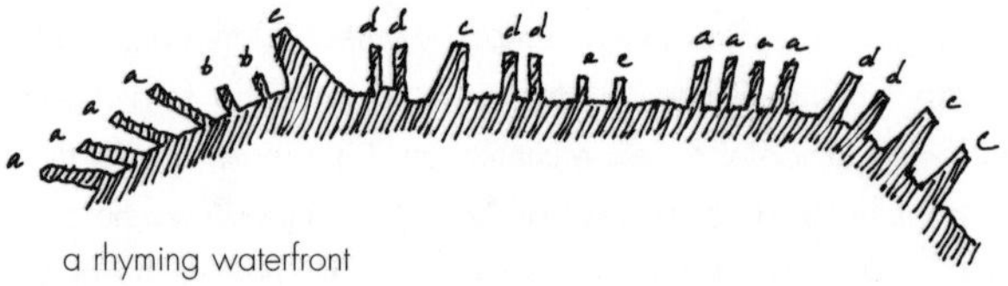

a rhyming waterfront

Meter divides the line of poetry into parts; it tells the voice how to read the poem by establishing a rhythm of stressed syllables. The number of stresses determines the number of feet in a line. (In the language of architecture, such parts are called *bays.)* The pattern of stresses and the number of parts in each line make up the meter. As an example, Shakespeare wrote his sonnets in *iambic pentameter*. An *iamb* is an unstressed syllable followed by a stressed one, as in the word un-*til*. *Penta* means five; an *iambic pentameter* line contains five iambic feet.

> Not from the stars do I my judgment plucke
> And yet me thinkes I have Astronomy.[57]

This simplest and most familiar of English meters sounds like a horse's trot (*anapestic* meter sounds like a canter), and graphically scans like this:

> / u u / u / u / u /
> u / u / u / u / u /

Often, as in this example, the first foot ("*Not* from") of the first line departs from the meter and begins with a stressed syllable—this gives the overall poem a bit more symmetry, and a more definitive start.

> *And miles to go before I sleep,*
> *And miles to go before I sleep.*
>
> Robert Frost, "Stopping by Woods on a Snowy Evening"

REPETITION IN POETRY EXCITES MULTIPLE READINGS, but it is perhaps the most under-appreciated virtue of good buildings. Contemporary architects often worry that their designs will be 'boring,' and compensate by distinguishing every feature of the program with unique form. As a result, our landscape is littered with buildings that seem noisy, hyperactive, and even neurotic.

Repetition is soothing, but hardly boring. Unlike the refrain of a song, which is a device clearly positioned to mark the different verses, repetition in a poem sets us up for delight in the small exceptions to it. Paz elucidates his concept of "variety within unity" when he writes: "What we call development is merely the alliance between repetition and surprise." [58]

T. S. Eliot conditioned us to the *sound* of repetition in "The Hollow Men:"

> This is the way the world ends,
> This is the way the world ends,
> This is the way the world ends
> Not with a bang but a whimper

and to the *idea* of repetition in "East Coker:" [59]

> You say I am repeating
> Something I have said before
> I shall say it again.
> Shall I say it again?

Repetition is both a tug and an anchor; it can work to pull time forward, or to slow time down. The latter effect drew Mark Stand to the villanelle form when he decided to write poems about two of de Chirico's paintings:

> The lines keep coming back, and in de Chirico's paintings you have the same things coming back, the flags, the towers, the boats, the trains, the shadows, long shadows. So I chose the form that I thought came closest to the paintings' spirit...I don't think a villanelle would work for many painters. I associated it specifically with de Chirico. [60]

The first repeating line of Strand's "The Disquieting Muses" is: "Boredom sets in first, and then despair." Both the meter and the content of this line echo the slow time of the painting. The other repeating line, "something about the silence of the square," complements the tempo of tedium by suggesting an ineffable sense of anticipation.

Architecture begins with the making of a room.
Louis Kahn

MODERN POETS WHO ARE NOT AFRAID TO WRITE IN STANZAS are like modern architects who are not afraid to design in rooms; there is nothing inherently archaic about either one. In Italian, the word stanza *means* room. Like a room, a stanza encloses an interior. The stanza is the most provocative visual quality of the poem, and inspires graphic representation.

Here are two quatrains, one written in the eighteenth century (William Blake, "The Tyger"), the other in the twentieth (W. H. Auden, "In Memory of W. B. Yeats"):

Tyger Tyger burning bright
In the forest of the night.
What immortal hand or eye
Dare frame thy fearful symmetry?

Earth receive an honored guest:
William Yeats is laid to rest.
Let the Irish vessel lie
Emptied of its poetry.

Except for one syllable (the unstressed "dare" at the beginning of Blake's fourth line) the meter is the same in both poems—each line is iambic, seven syllables, and begins and ends with a stress. Even more striking, the rhyme scheme of each is *aabb*, and "eye–symmetry" and "lie–poetry" show the same slanted rhyme.[61] If a stanza is defined by its number of lines, its meter, and its rhymes, these two 'rooms' are nearly identical:

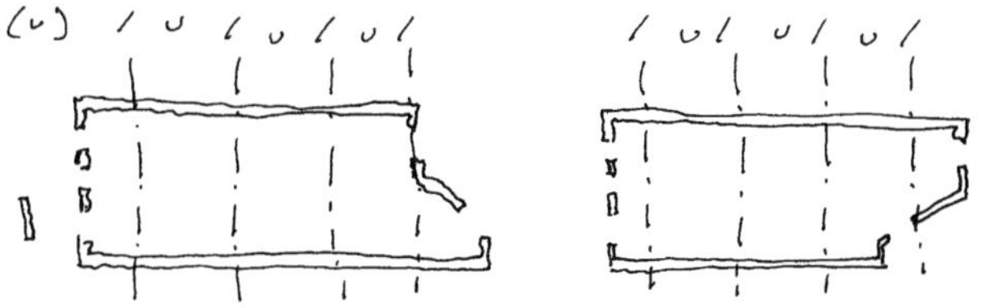

'Closed forms' in poetry are most recognizable in the structure and number of their stanzas. In order to more fully explicate the tectonic implications of poetry,

I have chosen to 'draw from' three stanzaic forms in addition to the villanelle: the *ballad,* the *sestina,* and the *pantoum.*[62]

THE BALLAD is one of the oldest forms of English poetry. Yet like other traditional forms it lends itself with astonishing versatility to modern adaptation, to being stripped of both ornament and sentiment. This ballad by Gwendolyn Brooks maintains the ballad's distinct function of narrative, but breaks the tradition of extended length. The poem still tells a story, but the story is as brief as the lives it describes; the form of the poem and its content are congruent.

WE REAL COOL

The Pool Players.
Seven at the Golden Shovel.

We real cool. We
Left school. We

Lurk Late. We
Strike Straight. We

Sing sin. We
Thin gin, We

Jazz June. We
Die soon.

There is probably no other poem in English in which all words are only one syllable, and all syllables are equally stressed. This poem contains no prepositions, no conjunctions, no articles; it is a poem without transitions or details. There is only one pronoun ('we' is also the speaking subject) that is repeated exactly the same number of times as there are lines in the poem. There are three rhymes, all of which are internal.[63] Strong consonants 'inhabit' the stanzas of the poem, first the *l*'s, then the *s*'s, finally the *j* sounds and the hard *d* at the end, only slightly softened by the sweet sound of *soon*.

"We Real Cool" balances itself like a slender building with cantilevers. The poem could not be more modern in the sense that it is absent of both ornament and hierarchy. Its structure may be drawn like this:

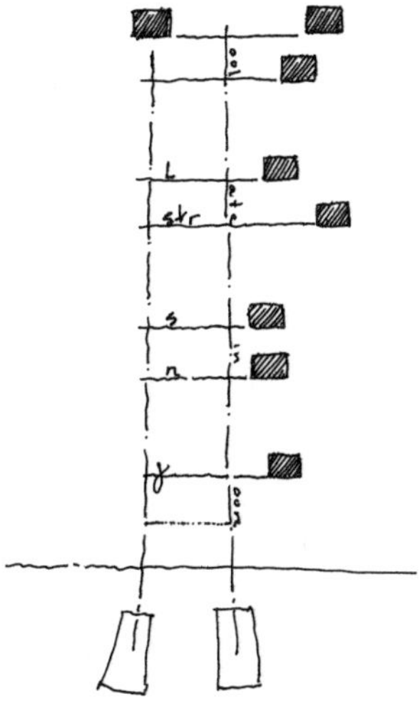

The ballad is historically a form with social content. At a time when the question of whether to embrace social agendas has divided the architectural profession into those concerned with a purity of form and those concerned with the human condition, this tough spare poem gives us a lesson in an economy of means that supports both.

THE SESTINA, like the villanelle, enjoyed a renaissance in the twentieth century. It has a precise architecture of six stanzas with six lines each, and an *envoi* of three lines at the end. Six unrhymed words at the end of each line reoccur in each stanza, in a strict pattern. On the facing page is a drawing of the poem "After the Trial" by Weldon Kees, and below is a word 'schedule' showing the order of the repeating words for each stanza.

LAST WORD	SENTENCE	GUILT	ROOMS	PARENTS	FOREVER	INNOCENCE
Stanza I	1	2	3	4	5	6
II	6	1	5	2	4	3
III	3	6	4	1	2	5
IV	5	3	2	6	1	4
V	4	5	1	3	6	2
VI	2	4	6	5	3	1

THE PANTOUM is a poem that repeats every line; its repetitions spiral slowly forward through an unspecified number of stanzas of four lines each. Here is a drawing of John Ashbery's poem "Pantoum":

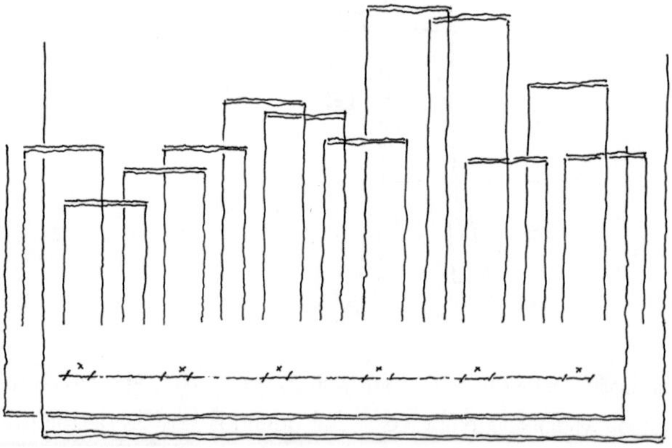

A teacher once told me (in defense of his preference for classical architecture) that it was more efficient to design a symmetrical building, since one only had to do half the work. The same could be said of writing a pantoum;

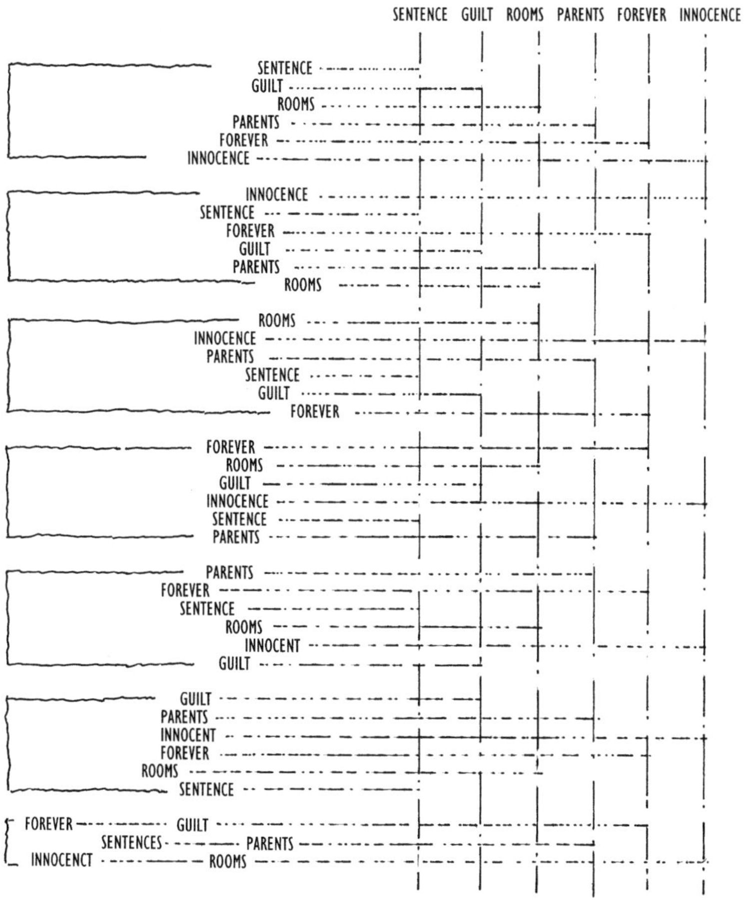

Weldon Kees, "After the Trial"

every line in the poem occurs exactly twice. The second occurrence is always three lines following the first; thus the steps of the dance are predictable. This creates a mesmerizing sense of *déjà vu* in the reading of the poem. The pantoum closes its spiral into a loop by repeating the first line as the last.

Oh Di! I have seen time curved around space, biting his tail.
Peter Schneeman, "Through the Finger Goggles"

THE VILLANELLE HAS PROVED POPULAR among modern poets choosing to experiment with a closed form; perhaps this is because its cyclical shape appealed to a century in which both time and space took on curvature. The space of the villanelle seems both infinite and hollow; it has none of the mass of the pantoum with its lumbering pace, or of the sestina with its stern and didactic repetitions of single words. Like a Gothic cathedral, the villanelle is an ideal form for exciting our emotions without the distraction of content.

Like cathedrals also, villanelles look deceptively alike until one becomes familiar with the details unique to each one. The form of the cathedral expresses the aspirations of a culture in stone; it is also an acoustic chamber for singing voices. The effect of the villanelle, write Mark Strand and Eavan Boland, is to "make an acoustic chamber for single words."[64] Rhyme and repetition collaborate to form this round spatial structure. In fact, it is generally believed that the form began as a seasonal tradition in the agrarian fields of Italy, where it was sung in 'rounds.'

Its 'specification' demonstrates that rhyme and repetition in the villanelle are intrinsic to its stanzaic structure. Of these, repetition contributes most fully to the construction of the 'acoustic chamber' for words. But even within this formal constraint, the poet can 'detail' the repeating line in a way that changes the pattern of enclosure. In Merrill's villanelle "The World and the Child," a change in syntax opens an unexpected doorway halfway through the last line of a stanza, with *"Awake"*:

> Their talk, mild variation, chilling theme,
> Falls on the child. Awake and wearied of
>
> Mere pain, mere wisdom also, he would have
> All the world waking from its winter dream,

Like the Barcelona Pavilion of Mies van der Rohe, one can enter this poem in many places:

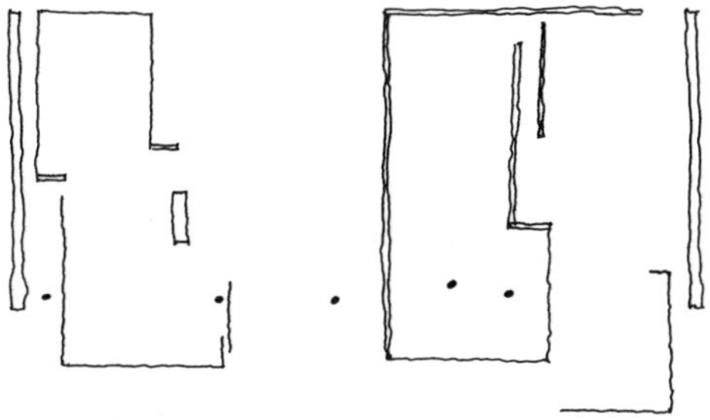

plan diagram: "The World and the Child"

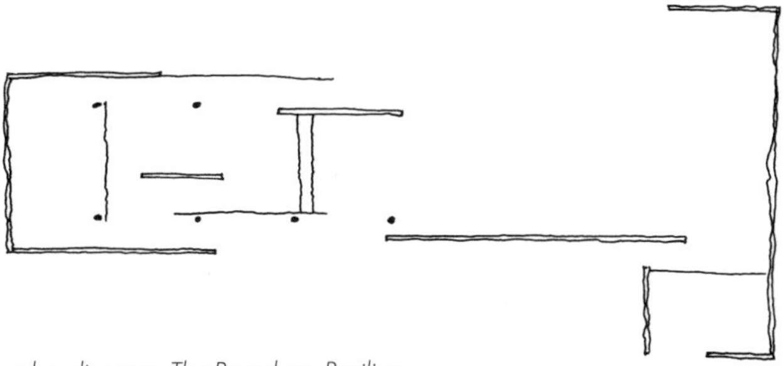

plan diagram: *The Barcelona Pavilion*

IN SECTION, the lines of a poem might act more like columns than like beams, and a sectional drawing of a villanelle expresses the metaphor of the "acoustic chamber" graphically. To appreciate this effect in the overlay drawings of the six villanelles throughout this book, turn the book 90° so that the lines of text run vertically up the page. View any of the drawings in this manner, and it becomes clear that the left margin of the poem acts as a foundation that holds up its form, while the rhyme scheme forms a complex and undulating roof.

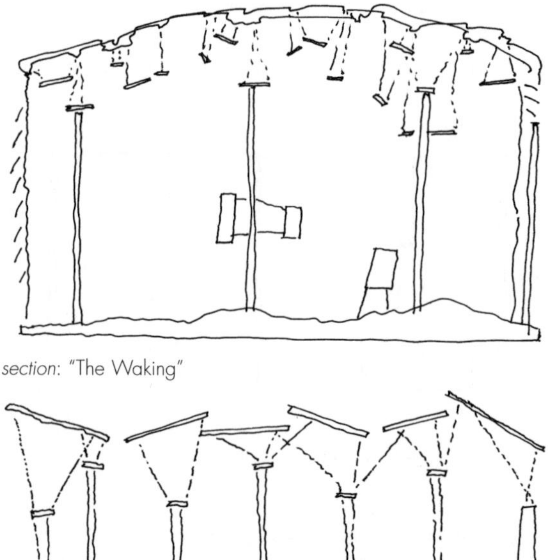

section: "The Waking"

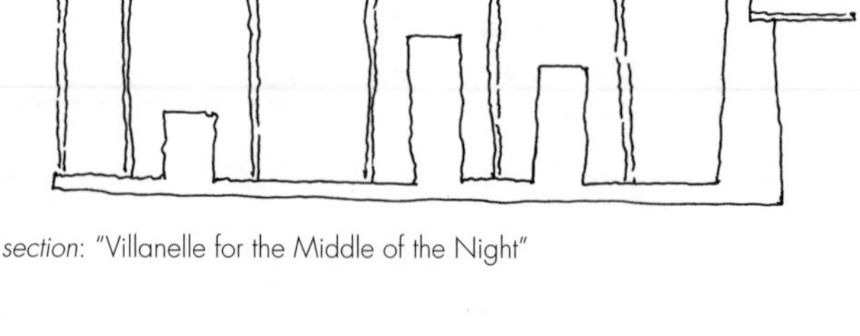

section: "Villanelle for the Middle of the Night"

IF WE MAKE A LEAP IN SCALE, the villanelle can be drawn as an urban plan; the words and lines make not columns or furniture or even rooms, but entire structures or blocks. The morphology of the poem creates a narrative space within which 'building types' reappear with measured frequency.

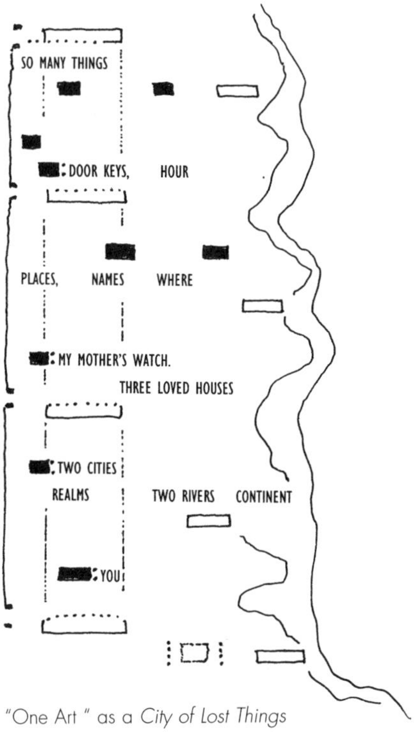

"One Art" as a *City of Lost Things*

The last poem in this collection is one of the best known villanelles in the English language: Theodore Roethke's "The Waking". The form of this poem is absolute, and its meaning is absolutely ambiguous. The relentless *iambic pentameter* works like a metronome; it measures time by describing time through space. The internal paradox of "wake to sleep" is as hypnotic as the weighty stones that seem to levitate Chartres Cathedral from its earth. Like Chartres, "The Waking" represents its type to perfection.

> *This so weighty metal, when it becomes the associate of a fancy, assumes the most active virtues of the mind. It has her restless nature. Its essence is to vanish.* [65]
>
> Paul Valéry, *Eupalinos or The Architect*

THE TWIN PARADOXES of the heaviness of words and the lightness of built form underscore the potentially rich dialogue between poems and buildings. Though Valéry is speaking of currency in its pure state, we might apply his theory of disappearance directly to architecture. It, more than any other art, needs that 'weighty metal' to exist; yet I would say that if architecture is to become meaningful again, it too must vanish.

The French word *calque*, meaning *to copy*, is the name of the transparent paper that architects in France use to make overlay drawings. In English we call this paper *trace*, and we understand that a tracing is not really a copy at all; it is an evolution, a transformation that sometimes manifests addition and sometimes erasure. In some sense each villanelle is a tracing of the ones that have been written before it; certainly it is *not* a copy. The copy does not acknowledge the passing of time, the trace does. We distrust the trace, particularly when it involves subtraction, because in some sense, the desire to hold time at bay is a motive for all art. But architecture has, in turn, confused ignorance of the past with a revolutionary present and trivial reminders of the past with meaningful memory. This 'romance of progress' and 'nostalgia for ruins' are both linear concepts, lines drafted in opposite directions against time's own measure, as if time were something we can either accept or reject at will. Such simplemindedness has both impoverished our landscape of meaning and filled it up with stuff.

While poetry at its best continues to make us think of poetry, architecture at its best cannot allow us think of architecture. Industry continues to tempt us with new products in wood, concrete and steel, but our primary building material is nearly weightless; in fact, it is air. Not only weightless but invisible, quixotic. Building space requires that we make our buildings empty. The villanelle as an 'acoustic chamber' is a suitable metaphor for what architecture can now become, because it so perfectly illustrates the ideal of emptiness.

SO HOW DO WE FIND the magic that makes a window hinge into a butterfly, the metaphysics that allows a curtain wall to drift like a curtain?

Answers are not
What the poem is about.

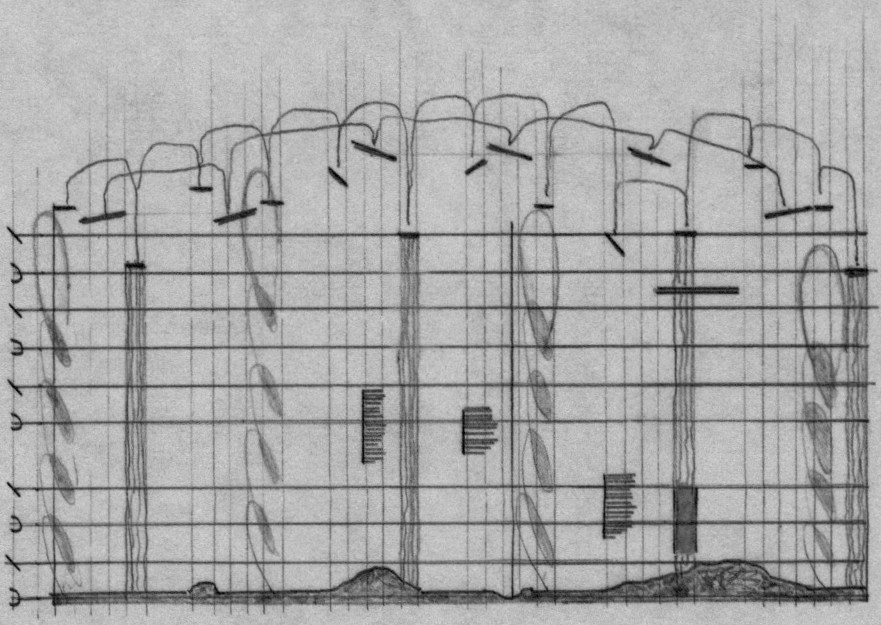

theodore Roethke, "The Waking"

JStone 2/2001

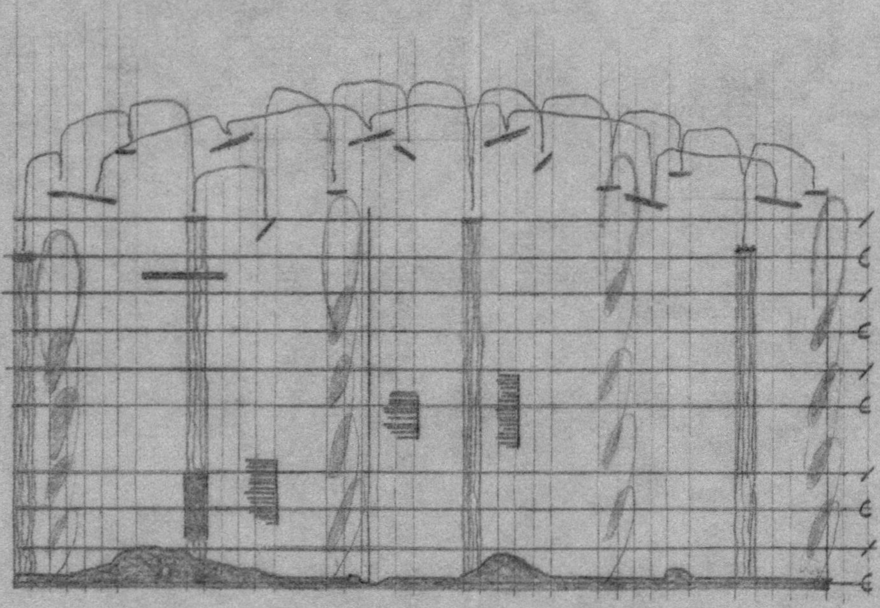

Theodore Roethke, "The Waking"

Theodore Roethke

THE WAKING

I wake to sleep, and take my waking slow.
I feel my fate in what I cannot fear.
I learn by going where I have to go.

We think by feeling. What is there to know?
I hear my being dance from ear to ear.
I wake to sleep, and take my waking slow.

Of those so close beside me, which are you?
God bless the Ground! I shall walk softly there,
And learn by going where I have to go.

Light takes the Tree; but who can tell us how?
The lowly worm climbs up a winding stair;
I wake to sleep, and take my waking slow.

Great Nature has another thing to do
To you and me; so take the lively air,
And, lovely, learn by going where to go.

This shaking keeps me steady. I should know.
What falls away is always. And is near.
I wake to sleep, and take my waking slow.
I learn by going where I have to go.

ENDNOTES

WHY POEMS

[1] Paul Valéry, "Problems of Poetry" in *The Collected Works of Paul Valéry*, volume 7: *The Art of Poetry*, trans. Denise Folliot (New York: Pantheon Books, 1958), p.98.

[2] In Valéry's dialogue *Eupalinos or The Architect,* Socrates and Phaedrus have an extended conversation about the unique relationship between architecture and music, which concludes:

> These are then two arts which enclose man in man; or, rather, which enclose the being in its work, and the soul in its acts and in the production of its acts, as our former body was was entirely enclosed in the creations of its eye, and surrounded with sight. By means of two arts it wraps itself up, in two different ways, in their inner laws and wills, which are figured forth in one material or another, stone or air.
> Valéry, *The Collected Works, volume 4: Dialogues*, p. 96

[3] The etymologies throughout *Poems for Architects* are derived primarily from the following sources: *The American Heritage Dictionary of Indo-European Roots*, ed. Calvert Watkins (Boston: Houghton Mifflin, 1985); Robert Claiborne, *The Roots of English* (New York: Times Books, 1989).

[4] Octavio Paz, "The Few and the Many" in *The Other Voice*, trans. Helen Lane, (New York: Harcourt Brace Jovanovich, 1991) p. 77.

[5] Lawrence Halprin, *The RSVP Cycles: Creative Processes in the Human Environment*, (New York: George Braziller, 1969) p. 7.

[6] Valéry, "Remarks on Poetry" in *The Art of Poetry*, p. 211.

[7] Valéry, "Poetry and Abstract Thought" in *The Art of Poetry,* p. 79.

[8] Le Corbusier, *Toward a New Architecture*, trans. Fredrick Etchells, (London: The Architectural Press, 1946), p. 89.

[9] For example, consider these two passages from Shakespeare's *Macbeth:*

> *death as a metaphor for sleep:*
> "The death of each day's life, sore labour's bath,
> balm of hurt minds…" (II:2)
> *sleep as a metaphor for death:*
> "…Duncan's in his grave
> After life's fitful fever he sleeps well." (III:2)

[10] From Charles Baudelaire, *"Correspondences"*: The relevant line of the poem in French is *"L'homme y passe à travers dés forêts de symboles."*

[11] *Rhizome* refers to a root structure that spreads like a web rather than like a tree. The rhizome as a metaphor for urban space became interesting to me when I read the following passage by Umberto Eco in the *Postscript to the Name of the Rose*:

> And finally there is the net, or, rather, what Deleuze and Guattari call "rhizome." The rhizome is so constructed that every path can be connected with every other one. It has no center, no periphery, no exit, because it is potentially infinite. The space of conjecture is a rhizome space.
> (trans. William Weaver, San Diego: Harcourt Brace Jovanovich, 1983, pp. 57)

[12] Valéry, "A Poet's Notebook" in *The Art of Poetry*, p. 187.
[13] *Scansion* is the graphic analysis of verse to show its meter. The word also means *the act of climbing*.
[14] In *The Making of a Poem* (New York: W. W. Norton, 2000), Mark Strand and Eavan Boland use the term "closed form" to denote formal structures of poetry.
[15] Strand, "On Becoming a Poet," in *The Weather of Words* (New York: Alfred A. Knopf, 2000) p. 51.

THE HOUSE WAS QUIET AND THE WORLD WAS CALM

Wallace Stevens was a favorite poet of architect Louis Kahn. Kahn misquoted Stevens in his AIA Gold Medal Acceptance Speech in Detroit on June 24, 1971:

> The great American poet Wallace Stevens prodded the architect, asking, 'What slice of the sun does your building have?' To paraphrase, what slice of the sun enters your room? [...] Stevens seems to tell us that the sun was not aware of its wonder until it struck the side of a building.
> Reprinted as "The Room, the Street and Human Agreement" in *AIA Journal 56* (September 1971): 33.

No such line exists in Stevens' work, but Kahn is probably referring to the line "Let us build the building of light" from Stevens' poem "Architecture," or these lines from another stanza of the same poem:

> How shall we hue the sun,
> Split it and make blocks,
> To build a ruddy palace?

POEMS AT HOME

[16] Henry David Thoreau, *Walden or Life in the Woods,* (New York: New American Library, 1960) p. 163.
[17] Adrienne Rich, "Vesuvius at Home: The Power of Emily Dickinson," in *Critical Essays on Emily Dickinson*, Paul J. Ferlazzo, ed. (Boston: G. K. Hall & Co., 1984), p. 175.
[18] Dickinson, in a letter to Thomas Higginson, *The Letters of Emily Dickinson*, ed. Thomas H. Johnson (Cambridge: Belknap Press, 1958)
[19] Dickinson, in a letter to Thomas Higginson, *The Letters of Emily Dickinson*.
[20] This is from the Williams poem "A Sort of a Song" in William Carlos Williams, *Selected Poems* (New York: New Directions, 1949):

> [...]Compose. (No ideas
> but in things) Invent!
> Saxifrage is my flower that splits
> the rocks.

[21] William Carlos Williams, "The Red Wheelbarrow" in *Selected Poems*, p. 36.

[22] Approximately since World War II, the word *home* has been co-opted by the real estate profession to mean *house*. Thus homes are built and bought; they are commodities, and in contemporary usage the word *house* barely exists. I would say that the semantic distinction is worth reinstating.
[23] Webster's Dictionary defines *oneiric* as *of or pertaining to dreams*. Bachelard's use of the word reveals his conviction that the house is above all a shelter for reverie.
[24] Gaston Bachelard, *The Poetics of Space*, New York, Beacon Press, 1958, p. 8.
[25] Bachelard, p. 47.
[26] Bachelard, p. 17–8. The entire first chapter "The House: From Cellar to Garret" explores this phenomenology of the house as a vertical dream world.
[27] Adrienne Rich, "Defying the Space that Separates" in *Arts of the Possible*, New York, W.W. Norton & Co., 2001, p. 109.

INVENTORY (original version in Spanish):

INVENTARIO
Hay que arrimar una escalera para subir. Un tramo le falta.
¿Qué podemos buscar en el altillo
sino lo que amontona el desorden?
Hay olor a humedad.
El atardecer entra por la pieza de plancha.
Las vigas del cielo raso están cerca y el piso está vencido.
Nadie se atreve a poner el pie.
Hay un catre de tijera desvencijado.
Hay unas herramientas inútiles.
Está el sillón de ruedas del muerto.
Hay un pie de lámpara.
Hay una hamaca paraguaya con borlas, deshilachada.
Hay aparejos y papeles.
Hay una lámina del estado mayor de Aparicio Saravia.
Hay una vieja plancha a carbón.
Hay un reloj de tiempo detenido, con el péndulo roto.
Hay un marco desdorado, sin tela.
Hay un tablero de cartón y unas piezas descabaladas.
Hay un brasero de dos patas.
Hay una petaca de cuero.
Hay un ejemplar enmohecido del Libro de los Mártires de Foxe, en intrincada letra gótica.
Hay una fotografía que ya pueda ser de cualquiera.
Hay una piel gastada que fue de tigre.
Hay una llave que ha perdido su puerta.
¿Qué podemos buscar en el altillo
sino lo que amontona el desroden?
Al olvido, a las cosas del olvido, acabo de erigir este monumento
sin duda menos perdurable que el bronce y que se confunde con ellas.

MENDING WALL

The English word *wall* comes from the Latin *vallus*, referring to the pointed stakes that were set side by side to protect an encampment. Thus, the word *wall* first referred to fences of wood.

CITY POEMS

[28] I am thinking in particular of novels like Franz Kafka's *The Castle*, Alain Robbe-Grillet's *In the Labyrinth*, and George Orwell's *1984*.

[29] William Wordsworth, "The Prelude" in *The Complete Poetical Works of William Wordsworth* (New York: Thomas Y. Crowell & Co., 1888 ed.).

[30] Wordsworth, "Composed upon Westminster Bridge, Sept. 3, 1802" in *The Complete Poetical Works.*

[31] Charles Baudelaire, "Crowds" in *Paris Spleen*, trans. Louise Varèse, (New York: New Directions, 1947; 1970 ed.) p. 20.

[32] Walter Benjamin, *The Arcades Project*, trans. Howard Eiland & Kevin McLaughlin, (Cambridge: Belknap Press, 1999). The sections of the project are called *convolutes*, and *Convolute J*, devoted to Baudelaire, is composed of one hundred fifty pages of entries. In separately published essays on Baudelaire, Benjamin further explores many of the themes contained in this *convolute*.

[33] Jean-Paul Sartre, *Baudelaire*, (Norfolk: New Directions, 1950) p. 181.

[34] Baudelaire, quoted in Benjamin, *The Arcades Project.*

[35] Baudelaire, quoted in Benjamin, *The Arcades Project.*

[36] Baudelaire, "Epilogue" in *Paris Spleen*, p. 108.

[37] Baudelaire described the relationship between his work and Poe's thus:

> The first time I ever opened a book by him and discovered, with rapture and awe, not only subjects which I had dreamt, but whole phrases which I'd conceived, were written by him twenty years before.
> (quoted in Enid Starkie, *Baudelaire*, (Norfolk: New Directions, 1958) p. 218.

[38] The French word *flâneur* is used now in English to denote the urban wanderer. Walter Benjamin disagrees with the equation between the *flâneur* and the man of the crowd; he writes:

> The man of the crowd is no flâneur. In him, composure has given way to manic behavior. Hence he exemplifies, rather, what had to become of the flâneur once he was deprived of the milieu to which he belonged.
> Benjamin, "On Some Motifs in Baudelaire" in *Illuminations*, (New York: Schocken Books, 1969) p. 172.

[39] Baudelaire, "Crowds" in *Paris Spleen*, p. 20.

[40] Osip Mandelstam, "What is the Name of This Street" in *Osip Mandelstam: 50 Poems*, trans. Bernard Meares, (New York: Persea Books, 1977).

[41] Thom Gunn, "Bringing to Light" in *Jack Straw's Castle*. For an extensive analysis of this poem relative to the urban underground, see Wendy Lesser, *The Life Below the Ground*,

(Boston: Faber & Faber, 1987) pp. 57–61.
[42] Baudelaire, in *Paris Spleen.*
[43] Merrill's poem resonates differently since September 11, 2001.
[44] The idea of the city as a place hospitable to wild things is developed at greater length in my essay "The Falcon's Return" in *Places* 12:3, p. 48–50.
[45] Benjamin, "Convolute M: The Flâneur" in *The Arcades Project,* p. 147.
[46] Italo Calvino, *Invisible Cities,* trans. William Weaver (New York: Harcourt Brace Jovanovich, 1980).
[47] Gabriel García Márquez, *One Hundred Years of Solitude,* trans. Gregroy Rabarsa (New York: Harper & Row, 1970).
[48] Jorge Luis Borges, "The Library of Babel" in *Labyrinths,* trans. James E. Irby (New York: New Directions, 1964).
[49] Benjamin, "On Some Motifs in Baudelaire" in *Illuminations,* p. 160.

PARIS

Corso is "naming" the city in terms of its writers rather than its buildings or streets. Artaud was a playwright, Rimbaud and Apollinaire were poets, and Hugo and Zola were novelists. "Montparnassian" refers to the area in the 14th *arrondissement* known as *Montparnasse,* which was the center of literary life in Paris before World War II.

LENINGRAD

In 1924 the name of the city was officially changed from St. Petersburg to Leningrad. This poem was written in December 1930, during Mandelstam's last attempt to settle in Leningrad; In 1991, the name was changed back to "Petersburg." "Dear guests" was a euphemism for the political police (from notes by translator Bernard Meares.)

TWO DE CHIRICOS

The two villanelles in this section were written as a pair, and are published in *Blizzard of One* under the title "Two De Chirico's" with subtitles for each of the two paintings. One poem was commissioned by the Art Institute of Chicago, which owns "The Philosopher's Conquest," and the other by the Museum of the University of Iowa, which owns one of the nineteen versions of "The Disquieting Muses."

A WALK THROUGH MUNICH (original version in Polish):

MARTWA NATURA
Chodze sobie po miescie,
czynszowe kamienice,
urzedowe budynki
postawione z marmuru,
oblozone bazaltem,
który rwalismy skalom
w Flossenburg, Matthausen, Lissa…
Patrze, mysle: benzyna,

troche recznych granatów
i kompania pracy,
tak sobie dom po domu,
ulica po ulicy,
dzielnica po dzielnicy,
jedno miasto po drugim,
tak jak w getcie w Warszawie,
jakby to bylo piekne dzielo architektury:
w górze—pogodne niebo,
w dole—spalone mury.

THE JAR & THE FIELD

Some of the themes in this essay are explored in two of my earlier publications: "The Jar and the Field" in *ACSA Conference Proceedings*, 1990, and "Camp and Field" in *Traditional Dwellings and Settlements Review*, 1991.

[50] Stephane Mallarmé wrote "Un Coup de Dés" near the end of his life as an experimental poem that shapes the text graphically on the page. The title line, "un coup de dés n'abolira jamais le hasard" is distributed through the entire poem, and interwoven with other texts in parallel. The title line translates: "A throw of the dice will never abolish chance."

[51] John Berger, "Field" in *About Looking*, (New York: Pantheon Books, 1980) pp. 197–8.

[52] Paul Klee, *Pedagogical Sketchbook*, (New York: Frederick A. Praeger, 1953) Introduction and translation by Sibyl Maholy-Nagy.

[53] Berger is quoted in Adrienne Rich's essay "Defying the Space That Separates," in *Arts of the Possible*, p. 107.

FIRST RULE OF SINHALESE ARCHITECTURE

I am indebted to Nick Ragouzis for his insight into the two ways that this poem may be read spatially:

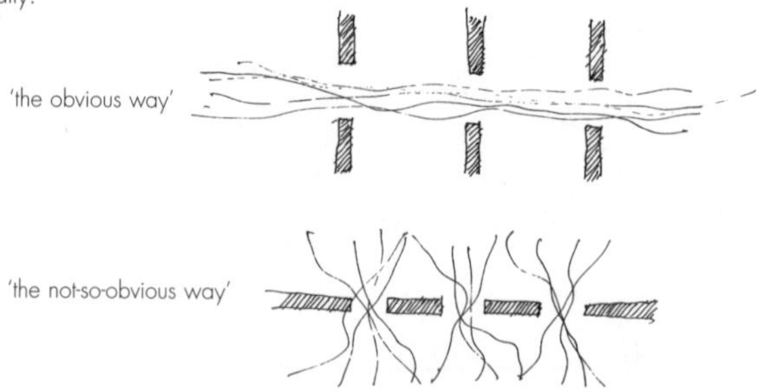

In the first diagram, the alignment of three doors "in a row" lets anyone pass through; in the second diagram, only the devil can so pass.

AFTER MALLARMÉ

This poem has special significance for me: my undergraduate thesis at New College was on the poetry of Mallarmé; twenty years later, my family bought a house in Bolinas, California that had been owned by Robert Creeley. Underneath layers of wallpaper in the tool shed, we uncovered this short "poem at home" written in Creeley's hand on the wood siding:

THE YARD BIRD
Patiently stumbling
Over familiar discontent
Lumbering Yardbird
Sings his lament.

THE CLEARING (original version in Swedish):

GLÄNTAN

Det finns mitt i skogen en oväntad glänta som bara kan hittas av den som gått vilse.

Gläntan är omsluten av en skog som kväver sig själv. Svarta stammar med lavarnas askgrå skäggstubb. De tätt sammanskruvade träden är döda ända upp i topparna där några enstaka gröna kvistar vidrör ljuset. Därunder: skugga som ruvar på skugga, kärret som växer.

Men på den öppna platsen är gräset underligt grönt och levande. Här ligger stora stenar, liksom ordnade. De måste vara grundstenarna i ett hus, jag kanske tar fel. Vilka levde här? Ingen kan ge upplysning om det. Namnen finns någonstans i ett arkiv som ingen öppnar (det är bara arkiven som håller sig unga.) Den muntliga traditionen är död och därmed minnena. Zigenarstammen minns men de skrivkunniga glömmer. Anteckna och glöm.

Torpet sorlar av röster, det är världens centrum. Men invånarna dör eller flyttar ut, krönikan upphör. Det står öde i många år. Och torpet blir en sfinx. Till slut är allt borta utom grundstenarna.

På något sätt har jag varit här förut, men måste gå nu. Jag dyker in bland snåren. Det går bara att tränga sig igenom med ett steg framåt och två åt sidean, som en schackspringare. Så småningom glesnar det och ljusnar. Stegen blir längre. En gångstig smyger sig fram till mig. Jag är tillbaka i kommunikationsnätet.

På den nynnande kraftledningsstolpen sitter en skalbagge i solen. Under de glänsande sköldarna ligger flygvingarna hopvecklade lika sinnrikt som en fallskärm packad av en expert.

SIX VILLANELLES

[54] Banister Fletcher, *History of Architecture According to the Comparative Method*, was first published in 1896 (New York: Charles Scribner's Sons) and is now in its 20th edition.

[55] For example, Henry Glassie, *Passing the Time in Ballymenone* (Indiana University Press, 1995). Glassie spent a year living in the village of Ballymemone, seeking the "variety within unity" in the poetry of daily village life. His book demonstrates, through both text and drawings, that the subtleties within such cultural typologies as rituals of work and placement of domestic furniture define a village's rich identity.

[56] I am indebted to David Buege, who first shared with me his theory of 'an architecture of simple volumes' in 1985.
[57] Shakespeare's "Sonnet XIV," (which lent its meter directly to "Farming Detroit")

> Not from the stars do I my judgment plucke,
> And yet me thinkes I have Astronomy,
> But not to tell of good, or evil lucke,
> Of plagues, of dearths, or seasons quallity;
> Nor can I fortune to breefe mynuits tell,
> Pointing to each his thunder, raine and winde,
> Or say with Princes if it shal go wel
> By oft predict that I in heaven finde.
> But from thine eies my knowledge I derive,
> And constant stars in them I read such art
> As truth and beautie shal together thrive
> If from thy selfe, to store thou wouldst convert:
> Or else of thee this I prognosticate,
> Thy end is Truthes and Beauties doome and date.

[58] Paz, *The Other Voice*, p. 9.
[59] T. S. Eliot's *Four Quartets* is made up of four long poems, "Burnt Norton" is one, "East Coker" is another.
[60] Strand in an interview with Ernie Hilbert in "Bold Type" on the Random House website: http://www.randomhouse.com/boldtype/0200/strand/interview.html.
[61] In a slant rhyme, the vowel sounds do not match, as in "ves-sel *lie* / po-e-*try*."
[62] For further discussion of the ballad, the sestina, and the pantoum, as well as many examples of each form, see Strand and Boland, *The Making of a Poem*. The authors refer to these poems as "closed forms;" other "closed forms" include the sonnet, the haiku, and the limmerick. Forms whose definition resides in content are called by Strand and Boland "shaping forms," and include the ode, the pastoral, and the elegy.
[63] *Internal rhyme* refers to rhyming words that do not fall at the ends of lines.
[64] Strand and Boland, *The Making of a Poem*, p. 20.
[65] Though "Eupalinos" was written in the twentieth century, Valéry freely mixes references from his own time with those from ancient Greece; thus we may assume that the "weighty metal" refers to gold.

BIOGRAPHICAL NOTES

Wynston H. Auden (1907–1973) was born in England, and at an early age received the Queen's Gold Medal for Poetry. Together with Pound and Eliot, he is acknowledged as one of the giants of modern poetry in English.

Wendell Berry is a national spokesperson for conservation and ecology, both through his poetry and in his teaching and prose writing. His most recent collection of essays is titled *Home Economics.*

Elizabeth Bishop (1911–1979) was one of the twentieth century American poets who best revived the use of closed forms like the villanelle. She was a close contemporary of Robert Lowell, who greatly admired her work.

Eavan Boland was born in Dublin, Ireland. She is the author of six volumes of poetry, and is coauthor with Mark Stand of *The Making of the Poem*. She teaches in the Department of English at Stanford University.

Jorge Luis Borges (1897–1984) is the author of short fables and poems that have become cornerstones of the genre of literature called 'magical realism.'

Tadeusz Borowski (1922–1951) was born in the Ukrainian town of Zytomierz. During the period of German occupied Poland he attended an underground university in Warsaw. All of his poems were written by the time he was twenty-four; in the last five years of his short life, he turned to fiction writing and journalism.

Gwendolyn Brooks (1917–2000) died while this book was being prepared. She was Poet Laureate of Illinois, and received a Pulitzer Prize for her book *Annie Allen*.

Gregory Corso (1930–2001) also died while this book was being prepared. A memorial service for him in Manhattan proclaimed him as "America's greatest lyric poet," to which Lawrence Ferlinghetti replied: "Corso was lyrical alright, but in a highly original, cutting sort of way." He was a talented painter as well as a poet.

Robert Creeley is a disciple of the late poet Charles Olsen, and taught with Olsen and Joseph Albers at Black Mountain College. He is the founder of the Black Mountain Review.

Rita Dove is a former Poet Laureate of the United States, and her book *Thomas and Beulah* won a Pulitzer Prize. She is currently Commonwealth Professor of English at the University of Virginia.

Robert Frost (1874–1963) is perhaps the most beloved of America's twentieth century poets. He wrote of the seasons and daily rhythms of New England life, and we might say he is to that landscape what Baudelaire is to Paris.

Thom Gunn was born in England, but has made his home in San Francisco. He is the recipient of a MacArthur Fellowship and the Lenore Marshall Poetry Prize of the American Academy of Poets.

Langston Hughes (1902–1967) began publishing poetry at the age of fifteen. As an eloquent spokesperson for the African American spirit and struggle, his belief that poetry is about risk is summed up in this line: "Hang yourself, poet, in your own words…Otherwise, you are dead."

André Kertész (1894–1985) was born in Budapest. His work spanned more than sixty years in a remarkable career that took him from his native Hungary to Paris and finally New York City, where he lived until his death.

Robert Lowell (1917–1977) attended Kenyon College and received the Pulitzer Prize for *Lord Weary's Castle* in 1947. He is perhaps the most celebrated of America's postwar poets.

A. A. Milne (1882–1956) was Scots by birth and spent his childhood in London. He is the author of the series of children's books that trace the lives and adventures of Winnie the Pooh, Christopher Robin, and all their friends.

Osip Mandelstam (1891–1938) produced his early poetry in Russia as one of the group of poets who called themselves "Acmeists." As a Soviet poet in the 1930's he was continually challenged for his political unorthodoxy, and was many times banished from Moscow and Leningrad, eventually to a camp near Vladivostok, where he died.

James Merrill (1926–1995) is the author of nine volumes of poetry collected under the title *From the First Nine*, and of the stunning long sequence *The Changing Light at Sandover*. He lived in Stonington, Connecticut.

Susan Mitchell's book *Rapture* was nominated for a National Book Award. She currently holds the Mary Blossom Lee Endowed Chair in Creative Writing at Florida Atlantic University.

Jacqueline Osherow is the author of four volumes of poetry and the recipient of fellowships from the Guggenheim Foundation and the National Endowment for the Arts. She teaches poetry at the University of Utah.

Sylvia Plath (1932–1963) was born in Jamaica Plain, Massachusetts and published her first poem when she was eight. She attended Smith College and won a Fulbright to study at Cambridge, England. In addition to several volumes of poems, she is the author of the autobiographical novel *The Bell Jar*.

Diana O'Hehir is Professor Emeritus of English at Mills College in Oakland, and is the author of two novels, *I Wish This War Were Over* and *The Bride Who Ran Away*, as well as several volumes of poetry. She lives in Bolinas, California.

Michael Ondaatje grew up in Sri Lanka, and moved to Canada in 1962. He writes fiction as well as poetry, and is perhaps best known for his novel *The English Patient*, which won the Booker Prize in 1992.

Ezra Pound (1885–1972) has been called "the inventor of modern poetry in English." During World War II, he was imprisoned in Pisa, Italy under suspicion of treason. The extent of his influence, largely through his major long work *The Cantos*, cannot be overstated.

Adrienne Rich is the author of over twenty books, including the volumes of poems *Snapshots of a Daughter-in-Law, Diving Into the Wreck*, and *The Atlas of a Difficult World*, and a recently published book of essays, *Arts of the Possible*.

Theodore Roethke (1908–1963) is best remembered as an extraordinary teacher. Many of his thoughts on teaching and poetry are contained in the volume published shortly after his death: *On Poetry and Craft*. Many of his poems explore the revival of closed forms.

Wallace Stevens (1910–1980) was an insurance executive in Hartford, Connecticut, and one of the most influential poets of the twentieth century. His poems were a source of inspiration for the architect Louis Kahn.

Mark Strand is a former Poet Laureate of the United States, and author of many volumes of poetry, including *Keeping Things Whole, Darker, The Continuous Life* and *Blizzard of One*, which won the Pulitzer Prize in 1999. He is currently on the faculty of the Committee for Social Thought at the University of Chicago.

Tomas Tranströmer is the author of many volumes of poetry in his native Sweden, and one of that country's leading literary figures. He is also a practicing psychologist and an accomplished pianist.

John Updike is best known for his novels of suburban America. His critical opinion of contemporary architecture is evident in his novels as well as his poems, and is the subject of several of his essays, including "Is New York City Inhabitable?" and "Can Architecture be Criticized?"

ACKNOWLEDGEMENTS

The author and publisher wish to thank the following for permission to reprint the poems in this collection:

"Prologue: The Birth of Architecture," "Up There" and "Down There" from W. H. AUDEN: COLLECTED POEMS by W. H. Auden, ©1976 by Edward Mendelson, William Meredith and Monroe K. Spears, Executors of the Estate of W. H. Auden. Used by permission of Random House, Inc. "The Wild" from COLLECTED POEMS: 1957–1982 by Wendell Berry, ©1985 by Wendell Berry. Reprinted by permission of North Point Press, a division of Farrar, Straus and Giroux, LLC. "One Art" from THE COMPLETE POEMS: 1927–1979 by Elizabeth Bishop, ©1979, 1983 by Alice Helen Methfessel. Reprinted by permission of Farrar, Straus and Giroux, LLC. "Hanging Curtains with an Abstract Pattern in a Child's Room" from OUTSIDE HISTORY: SELECTED POEMS 1980–1990 by Eavan Boland, ©1990 by Eavan Boland. Used by permission of W. W. Norton & Company, Inc. "Inventory" from THE GOLD OF THE TIGERS by Jorge Luis Borges, translated by Alastair Reid, ©1976, 1977 by Alastair Reid, ©1972, 1975 by Emece Editores, S. A., Buenos Aires. Used by permission of Dutton, a division of Penguin Putnam Inc. "We Real Cool" from SELECTED POEMS by Gwendolyn Brooks. "Paris" from GASOLINE by Gregory Corso, ©1958 by Gregory Corso. Used by permission of City Lights Publishing. "After Mallarmé" from COLLECTED POEMS OF ROBERT CREELEY, 1945–1975 by Robert Creeley, ©1983 by the Regents of the University of California. Used by permission of The University of California Press granted on behalf of the author, Robert Creeley. "Geometry" from THE YELLOW HOUSE ON THE CORNER, Carnegie-Mellon University Press ©1980 by Rita Dove. Reprinted by permission of the author. "The Mending Wall" from THE POETRY OF ROBERT FROST edited by Edward Connery Lathem, ©1969 by Henry Holt & Co., LLC. Reprinted by permission of Henry Holt & Co., LLC. "Diagrams" and "Iron Landscapes" from COLLECTED POEMS by Thom Gunn, ©1994 by Thom Gunn. Reprinted by permission of Farrar, Straus and Giroux, LLC. "Empty House" from THE COLLECTED POEMS OF LANGSTON HUGHES by Langston Hughes, ©1994 by The Estate of Langston Hughes. Used by permission of Alfred A. Knopf, a division of Random House, Inc. "Baudelaire 2. Recollection" from HISTORY by Robert Lowell, ©1973 by Robert Lowell. Reprinted by permission of Farrar, Straus and Giroux, LLC. "Leningrad" by Osip Mandelstam appears in OSIP MANDELSTAM: 50 POEMS, translated by Bernard Meares, ©1977 by Bernard Meares. Reprinted by permission of Persea Books, Inc. (New York). "An Urban Convalescence" and "The World and the Child" from SELECTED POEMS 1946–1985 by James Merrill, ©1992 by James Merrill. Used by permission of Alfred A. Knopf, a division of Random House, Inc. "Halfway Down" by A. A. Milne, from WHEN WE WERE VERY YOUNG by A. A. Milne, illustrations by E. H. Shepard, ©1924 by E. P. Dutton, renewed 1952 by A. A. Milne. Used by permission of Dutton Children's Books, an imprint of Penguin Putnam Books for Young Readers, a division of Penguin Putnam Inc. "Venice" from EROTIKON by Susan Mitchell, ©2000 by Susan Mitchell. Reprinted by permission of HarperCollins Publishers, Inc. "House," "Home" and "The Retarded Children Find a World Built Just for Them" by Diana O'Hehir, from THE POWER TO CHANGE GEOGRAPHY, ©1979 by Princeton University Press. Reprinted by permission of Princeton University Press. "The Old Lady Under the Freeway" by Diana O'Hehir, reprinted from SUMMONED: POEMS by Diana O'Hehir, by permission of the University of Missouri Press, ©1976 by Diana O'Hehir. "The First Rule of Sinhalese Architecture" from HANDWRITING by Michael Ondaatje, ©1998 by Michael Ondaatje. Used by permission of Alfred A. Knopf, a division of Random House, Inc. "Villanelle for the Middle of the Night" from WITH A MOON IN TRANSIT by Jacqueline Osherow, ©1996 by Jacqueline Osherow. Used by permission of Grove/Atlantic, Inc. "I Am Vertical" from CROSSING THE WATER by Sylvia Plath, ©1965 by Ted Hughes. Reprinted by permission of HarperCollins Publishers, Inc. "In a Station of the Metro" by Ezra Pound, from PER-

SONAE, ©1926 by Ezra Pound. Reprinted by permission of New Directions Publishing Corp. "Boundary" and "In the Wake of Home" from THE FACT OF A DOORFRAME: Poems Selected and New, 1950–1984 by Adrienne Rich, ©1984 by Adrienne Rich. ©1975, 1978 by W. W. Norton & Company, Inc, ©1981 by Adrienne Rich. Used by permission of the author and W. W. Norton & Company, Inc. "The Waking," ©1953 by Theodore Roethke, from THE COLLECTED POEMS OF THEODORE ROETHKE by Theodore Roethke. Used by permission of Doubleday, a division of Random House, Inc. "The House Was Quiet and the World Was Calm" from COLLECTED POEMS by Wallace Stevens, ©1947 by Wallace Stevens. Reprinted by permission of Alfred A. Knopf, a Division of Random House, Inc. "Anecdote of the Jar" from COLLECTED POEMS by Wallace Stevens, ©1923 and renewed 1951 by Wallace Stevens. Reprinted by permission of Alfred A. Knopf, a Division of Random House, Inc. "The Curtains in the House of the Metaphysician" from THE COLLECTED POEMS OF WALLACE STEVENS by Wallace Stevens, ©1954 by Wallace Stevens. Used by permission of Alfred A. Knopf, a division of Random House, Inc. "Eating Poetry," "The Tunnel," "Keeping Things Whole," "Black Maps," by Mark Strand, ©1977 and 1985 by Mark Strand; "The Philosopher's Conquest" and "The Disquieting Muses" © by Mark Strand. "The Clearing" by Tomas Tranströmer, translated by Robert Bly, from TRUTH BARRIERS by Tomas Tranströmer, translated by Robert Bly, ©1980. Reprinted by permission of Robert Bly. "Suburban Madrigal," "São Paulo," and "L. A." from COLLECTED POEMS 1953–1993 by John Updike, ©1993 by John Updike. Used by permission of Alfred A. Knopf, a division of Random House, Inc.

ABOUT THE ILLUSTRATIONS

All overleaf photographs are by André Kertész, from the book *On Reading*, New York: Grossman, 1971, reprinted by permission of the Kertész Foundation. They are as follows:

Overleaf to:

WHY POEMS	*Newtown, CT, Sept 12, 1959*
POEMS AT HOME	*Hospice de Beaune, France, 1929*
CITY POEMS	*Venice, Sept 21, 1963*
THE JAR & THE FIELD	*Bellevue Forest, Paris, 1931*
SIX VILLANELLES	*Esztergom, Hungary, 1915*
INDEX	*New York City, July 30, 1969*

All drawings are by Jill Stoner. Drawings that overlay poems are pencil and gesso on mylar; drawings that accompany the essay "Six Villanelles" are ink on paper.

DE
VOLTAIRE,
EDITION,
augmentée,
de Figures en taille-douce.
TOME XI
DCC. LI.

INDEX BY TITLE & FIRST LINE

INDEX BY NAME

The text of this book is set in Futura Light, a font which uses very little ink. To my eye it most closely manifests the direction in which architecture must go.

J.S.